mission-shaped
and rural

mission-shaped
and rural

growing churches in the countryside

Sally Gaze

CHURCH HOUSE
PUBLISHING

Church House Publishing
Church House
Great Smith Street
London SW1P 3NZ

Tel: 020 7898 1451
Fax: 020 7898 1449

ISBN-13   978-0-7151-4084-0
ISBN-10   0 7151 4084 1

Published 2006 by Church House Publishing

The opinions expressed in this book are those of the
author and do not necessarily reflect the official policy
of the General Synod or The Archbishops' Council of
the Church of England.

Cover design by ie Design

Printed by MPG Books Ltd
Bodmin, Cornwall

Contents

Contents

Series introduction

In adopting and commending the *Mission-shaped Church* report, the Church of England took an important step forward in its understanding of God's mission. It is a journey full of opportunities and challenges, and one which opens up new questions. This series of titles is designed to resource thinking, reflection and action as the journey continues.

Each title in the *Mission-shaped* series considers how the principles presented in *Mission-shaped Church* can be applied in different areas of the Church's life and mission – in work with children and young people, in rural areas, in the parish church and in the area of apostolic spirituality. What perspectives and inner values are necessary to be part of a mission-shaped Church today? These areas were touched upon in the MSC report but are now explored in more depth.

All the authors write with the benefit of years of practical experience. The real-life case studies and practical examples they provide are designed both to be inspirational models of ministry and mission and to be adapted by the reader for their own context.

The examples cited include both 'fresh expressions', developed as a response to the culture of a particular group of people, and more traditional models, reflecting the fact that 'there are many ways in which the reality of "church" can exist'.[1] This series is firmly committed to advocating a mixed economy model for the Church of the future.

---

[1] Archbishop Rowan Williams, from the Foreword to *Mission-shaped Church*, GS 1523, Church House Publishing, 2004.

Dedication and acknowledgements

To a wonderful catalyst of rural inculturation – Chris, my husband and best friend, without whose enthusiasm and support this book would never have been written.

I would also like to express deep thanks to many other people who have given invaluable help:

Phil Wood, David Sochon, David Lancaster, Vicky Ball, church wardens, cell leaders and friends in the Tas Valley Benefice have given practical support in ministry which enabled me to find time to write.

The Right Revd David Atkinson, Paul Bayes, George Lings and the staff of the Sheffield Centre have generously engaged with the text, advised on research, encouraged and challenged me. Kathryn Pritchard, as editor, has much improved the style and shape of the book, and the Church Commissioners have patiently answered many technical enquiries.

Last, but not least, I wish to thank all who have allowed me to share their stories in this book and especially the people of the Tas Valley. I have learned so much from them. I am sure their stories will inspire many others.

Foreword

This is a book that deserves a readership beyond those who are already engaged in the mission-shaped agenda. It seeks to bring together sociological analysis and theological reflection on the rural church, together with a host of real-life illustrations of experimental patterns of church life. It was only the day before yesterday that people often claimed the strength of the Church of England was found in the countryside. Those who know rural England really well rarely claim such a thing now, though they are often conscious that without the Church of England Christian witness in the English countryside would be immensely impoverished. The rural church has had to endure radical reductions in clerical manpower in the past generation, well illustrated in the author's own benefice. This book illustrates that the result of such change can be to enable a new spirit of adventure in mission.

The Tas Valley benefice of six parishes, with a population of around 4,000, gives Sally Gaze plenty of experience of the sort of rural ministry that often seems focused on church buildings, regular worship, fundraising and community activities. But since her arrival in the benefice in September 2002 she has developed fresh ways of connecting local people with the gospel, well described here. She acknowledges the fragility of this work but traditional churches are often fragile too. It is only that we sometimes fail to see it, since our buildings are so solid and don't look like temporary structures for a pilgrim people.

Sally has written a work in progress, and this work is all the more valuable for that. Our participation in God's mission to his world often seems incomplete, frustrating and easily knocked off course. This side of the establishment of the kingdom of God it always will be. But it is also exhilarating and thrilling. God calls us and trusts us to find him in people and places where he has been undiscovered and unacknowledged. Sally captures both the excitement and the frustrations of being shaped by God's mission. That's because she writes from the perspective of the general practitioner in mission and ministry. But she's an adventurer too, and in the adventure of mission this book will prove a beneficial companion.

Graham James
Bishop of Norwich

About the book

> It will not do in our mission to assume that evangelism and
> the routine of worship in the countryside can or should be a
> straight transfer from urban, let alone suburban, patterns; some
> of the malaise and frustration that are felt in rural churches
> have to do with this, as well as with expectations that are
> brought in from elsewhere.[1]
>
> Archbishop Rowan Williams

Some days you could be excused for thinking that the *Mission-shaped Church*
report was all about urban and suburban situations. There are lots of stories
of exciting, resource-hungry, big projects, with dedicated teams of professionals that seem so far from the rural situation that country people like me feel
we could never emulate them.

But of course being mission-shaped is not about jumping onto somebody
else's bandwagon. It is about being shaped by God's mission – in the case of
this book, being shaped by God's heart of mission for rural people.

This book aims to give insights into the current issues in rural England as we
seek to wrestle with new understandings of what it means to be church in
this context. I hope that whether your involvement is at the national,
diocesan or local level you will find it useful as we look at:

- the nature of mission with especial reference to the rural situation;

- the nature of rural culture and cultural change in the countryside;

- ways for the Church to engage with rural culture;

- examples of rural fresh expressions of church;

- how to tell whether a fresh expression is really church;

- how to help rural fresh expressions grow to maturity;

- pruning the things which inhibit mission in the countryside;

- how old and new forms of church can work together for the glory of God.

Behind the book there also lies a personal story of what God has been teaching me, especially through the people of the Tas Valley where I minister. The Prologue tells something of that story which shows how many of the issues addressed in this book arise in a practical context.

Prologue: 'Doing different' – work in progress in one rural group of churches

'What about the church?'

It was the last session of a Christian basics course in the autumn of 2003. The title of the session was 'What about the church?'

There were seven young mums on the course from four different villages, drawn together by common mums-and-toddlers activities as well as a desire to find out more about the Christian faith. Five of them had made a definite commitment to follow Christ over the last few weeks. But only one of them had started to attend church regularly on a Sunday. To nearly all of them church was still a bit of a mystery:

'I quite like it when I go,' said one, 'as long as the children aren't with me making a noise . . . But I don't know the hymns and I don't know what to do when you do that thing up at the altar.'

'The thing is, my husband doesn't want to come,' says another, '– and Sunday is the only day we spend together as a family – I don't want him to resent me going.'

'I know what you mean', says a third. 'Also – the services in our village are very old-fashioned – I can just about manage to follow it but there's a lot I don't understand and I couldn't invite anyone else . . . I suppose I ought to be going to church but I get more out of coming here.' These young women easily identified with the presentation about what church means, about what church is for. Clearly, being part of God's family means that meeting together is not an optional extra . . . But there was a credibility gap: the course spoke of worship, fellowship, supporting each other, learning from God's word, mission and service. In the churches they knew there seemed to be other unofficial requirements – an interest in medieval church buildings, flower arranging or seventeenth-century English or being available at 11 a.m. on a Sunday morning to name but a few. There was palpable relief when I said that these things were just optional extras – not necessary parts of being in God's family. Yet, they and I knew that I could not offer them a congregation to join where the ideals of the gospel could be lived out without a fair amount of what would be to them off-putting baggage.

The Tas Valley Benefice is typical of many multi-parish benefices in accessible countryside. Each village focuses its church life around a weekly service of worship – some in modern language; some following the traditional *Book of Common Prayer* (1662). Any of the parish congregations in the Tas Valley would welcome them and their children with open arms – but the mums would be intensely aware of trying to keep their children quiet during the service. Even after the service, they would be likely to be invited to join the PCC fundraising committee before they were able to have conversations or times of prayer, which would help them in their deep searching.

In many respects, I knew that this little group had much in common with forms of church in the New Testament. In this group we had shared and prayed about deep personal grief, worries about children and supporting friends in horrific circumstances. We had struggled to engage with the Bible over the noise of ten toddlers and we had changed and grown. We had begun to think about mission by starting some events for parents with young children. We had begun to love each other.

So where would we go from here? If these young women and their children were going to be part of church in a way that was going to help them grow as disciples, we were going to have to do something different from what was available on a Sunday.

Doing different

If you have ever spent much time in Norfolk, you will have heard the old saying which expresses our county pride: 'In Norfolk, we dew diffrunt.' It means that Norfolk people are not apt to accept that they should do something just because everyone else does or because that's the way it's always been done.

I had been struck by this can-do attitude at my very first meeting with the twelve churchwardens when I became rector in 2002. We had been talking about teenagers in church. 'How are we going to make our services more appealing to them?' was the question.

We looked at the little we could do. We could worship with simple clear language, easy to follow worship cards and more modern music. Still, we knew that however hard we tried we simply would never be able to go far enough to make village worship 'cool' in youth terms. They would always feel that coming to church was coming into a foreign culture. The most important thing congregation members could do to help them was love them. I shared a picture I had of a youth congregation. Young people leading worship in their own style – not having to compromise with the needs of older generations; a safe place for them to grow in discipleship. I thought there might be horror at the idea of 'losing' the few teenaged attendees they had. Instead there was enthusiasm. They had been released from the impossible task of keeping everyone happy. One added, 'Instead of them coming to us to learn to worship our way, some of us would love to go to them and worship their way.'

This is the spirit of Norfolk 'dewing diffrunt'. There is more than one way of cracking a nut. There are potentially many more ways than one way of doing church in rural England today. A youth congregation is still some way off for us, but from Spring 2003, another way of 'doing different' had already taken off in the Tas Valley. In January 2003, several young people and over 20 adults had participated in an *Alpha* (Christian basics) course. Afterwards, the same question had occurred as for the group of young mums. Some would fit easily in to congregational life and Bible studies. But some needed a more intimate, less formal way of being church, which enabled them to keep asking questions. In response to these needs, we had started two cells.

Celling it in the Tas Valley

Every human body has cells, which multiply. Why not the body of Christ? I'd read a fair bit about something called 'cells' operating in big urban churches and often thought how well suited the idea seemed to be to the rural environment. Cell church is a 'church without walls' composed of small groups (6–14 members in each), meeting in people's homes during the week. As more people become disciples of Jesus, the idea is that the cells 'multiply' keeping each group small and intimate by increasing the number of cells. Cells are different from the familiar Bible studies / house groups in one essential respect: house groups are an addition to Sunday church, mainly for those who want to go deeper. Cells seek to be 'church-in miniature'. As such, they don't only engage in fellowship, Bible-study and prayer, but also in worship and the practical service and evangelism which are part of God's mission.

As people were becoming Christians through *Alpha* courses and weren't always immediately comfortable with congregational forms of church, this seemed to be an ideal way forward. In addition, it could complement rather than compete with the parish churches and would enable those who cannot regularly get to a Sunday service to be fully involved in the life of a local church. Two adult cells and one youth cell were started. By the time the young mums' *Alpha* course ended, the obvious thing seemed for it to become a daytime cell.

So the daytime cell began and soon became engaged in two very significant forms of outreach to their own network of parents of babies and toddlers. First, they became the core, which supported a new toddlers' music group held in the church room of one of the churches. This was not a particularly religious group, but a way of sharing Jesus' love practically by giving parents / carers a chance to get out and have fun together with their children. Secondly, they started a new worship service.

Worship '4All'

Some of the group lived in a small village called Swainsthorpe where only half a dozen older folk attended a *Book of Common Prayer* service each Sunday. There had been attempts to start a regular family service in the recent past, but it only really worked on special occasions. I was wary of putting in a lot of effort into a service that people might not attend. Any initiative would have to be a team effort and not me, alone. Several mums prayed about it and went to look at what others were doing in another Norfolk village, Southrepps. We received the warmest of welcomes from vicar David Bartlett and the whole church family. Their service had been started to complement the existing monthly 'Open Door' children's club held at 4.30 p.m., once a month on a Sunday in one of the other villages in the team. The style was informal and interactive. Our children loved it and yet, it wasn't too flashy. The most important ingredients appeared to be love and food.

In February 2004, our own '4All' service was born. Roughly 25 adults and 25 children (mostly under five) came to join in. The liturgy is from *Common Worship* – but in its very simplest form. Music is provided via backing tracks and a CD player. It consists of a mixture of contemporary worship songs, very well known hymns and wild and wacky children's songs known to the children through holiday clubs and school assemblies. Children often act out the Bible reading. The Ministry of the Word is about testimony and story – an emphasis on applying God's word to our lives, rather than explanation and analysis. Craft activities are prepared by one of the cell members and often form the basis of prayers. We hope the service is able to be understood by those with no knowledge of the Christian faith and some non-believing parents bring their children in order that they may have some knowledge of Christianity to make informed choices of their own. The liturgy ends with saying grace for the shared tea, so the food is an integral part of the service and most of the congregation help to provide the food which is often very imaginative. We've had star-shaped biscuits at Christmas and fish sandwiches when learning about the story of the miraculous catch. Attendance is between 30 and 50 participants, nearly all of whom now have some sort of active role in preparing for the service. The cell members pray for all those who attend when we plan the service and the '4All' crowd is becoming a little community. This includes not only cell members, but people from Swainsthorpe who previously did not regularly attend church, and folk from other villages for whom the afternoon time and informal style suits their young children.

Growing a new church alongside the old

In effect, what is happening with the cells and their initiatives like '4All' is that a new kind of church is growing alongside the old. True, it is a very young fragile kind of church. There are plenty of ups and downs. My worries that it will all fall apart are a great inspiration to prayer. But there is nothing like a rural multi-parish benefice to help you see church in the small and fragile. Within one multi-parish benefice, we have a microcosm of the challenge of what Rowan Williams calls the 'mixed economy':

> We have to ask whether we are capable of moving towards a 'Mixed Economy', recognising church where it appears and having the willingness and skill to work with it.[1]

In my own mind, I was convinced cells had the marks of being church from the beginning. They worshipped and loved, they related to the wider church and respected the authority of its ordained leaders and participated in the sacraments, they studied the Bible, they engaged in mission. Some of our churches meet only for an hour a week on a Sunday and have less than a dozen active members. If they are church, how could the gathered cells not be church? In terms of weekly attendance, they were soon as strong as any of the parish churches in the benefice. However, there seemed to be no way for them to achieve official status within the Church of England structures because they had no building – but hadn't I spent a lot of my ministry teaching that church is about people not buildings? – and here was the proof.

As the cells grew, it was clear to me that we needed to give them sufficient responsibility to help them grow up. In addition, the wardens and ministry team needed to have a clear idea of where they fitted into the structures of the benefice. The obvious solution might be to put them under one of the PCCs, but it was difficult to see which one of the six PCCs they should relate to. Their membership was not, and is not, based on geographical parishes. Instead it is based on networks of friends and times when people are available to meet. One cell might have members in it who also attend three different parish churches as well as some for whom the cell was their only form of church membership. Coming under the umbrella of one of the PCCs was not an option. There is no mother church or minster church in our benefice with natural oversight of smaller churches. For a network church covering the team, to be structurally part of one of the PCCs would have led to misunderstanding and an undermining of the vision to reach networks of people who do not necessarily relate to a parish church.

I began to think about the work of Henry Venn. Henry Venn was a great missionary thinker in the nineteenth century. He talked about how three things were necessary for new churches to grow to maturity. They needed to be self-governing, self-financing and self-propagating.[2] The cells were already self-propagating, in fact far more so than any of the parish churches. But there were real obstacles to them becoming self-governing and self-financing. They had no legal standing within the Church of England. If I were to leave as rector, they could be closed down by my successor. They had no funds of their own and could not contribute directly to the benefice share. Those members for whom cell was their sole church had no easy way of giving. I was becoming aware that financial dependence on the parish churches was hindering the new cell members from taking the stewardship aspects of discipleship seriously. I saw the cell church suddenly like a young teenager needing to be given more responsibility and recognition in order to be able to grow to maturity and take its place alongside the parish churches within the team.

Gradually, gradually, we are working with our area bishop, David Atkinson, and other senior staff to find a way for this baby church to have comparable status to the parish churches in the team. In 2005, a cell bank account was set up and the cell church paid a small contribution to the benefice share. Our parish share number has a disproportionate importance for it gives the cell church a definite identity within the diocese until such time as network churches can be properly recognized within the Church of England.

Meanwhile, the cells and the parish churches in the benefice do not merely complement each other; an unlooked-for synergy has been created. I had looked to the cells to plug the gaps the parish churches were failing to reach, but a by-product of this is that new bridges have been created by which people have found their way into parish churches. This is most obvious in the case of the '4All' service but other congregations have also experienced growth when new Christians, having gained confidence through the cells, then also begin to attend congregational worship. The most committed members of our PCCs are frequently also cell members. In this way, the existence of benefice cells has increased inter-parish understanding and co-operation across the benefice in matters such as children's work.

The story of the Tas Valley shows how engaging in mission in the rural context sometimes means church-planting. It also shows the importance of existing parish churches in mission. What unites both old and new is a common starting-point – the Mission of God himself. It is this which we turn to consider in Chapter 1.

Mission

Mission-shaped church or church-shaped mission?

 ### The parable of the would-be farmer

Once upon a time, the Lord of the Manor saw great potential in one of the young men living on his estate and called him into his office. 'Come and farm for me,' he said.

The young man was very excited about his vocation and went to study at agricultural college where they taught him all sorts of things such as farm history, farm doctrine and pasture care. He thought it strange that harvest and food supply was such a small part of the curriculum, but he had read some good books and remained confident.

Eventually he took up his first post. But he somehow felt that things were not quite what he had expected. He had six farm buildings each of which had to be managed separately with their own farmyard, paperwork and Poultry, Cattle and Crops meetings (known in farming circles as PCCs). These farms were on part of the manoral lands with a rich history, and the buildings were medieval and required a lot of maintenance. He hadn't expected to have to do as much paperwork, spend as much time maintaining farm buildings or have as many meetings. When would there be time for actual farming?

So the paperwork blossomed and grew; the building maintenance blossomed and grew and the meetings blossomed and grew. Many seeds were planted and some blossomed and grew, but there never seemed enough time for harvesting the crop and even less was taken to market. The farmer hoped that someone else would do the harvesting later, but in his heart he suspected that most of the crop would never be gathered in and would simply go to waste.

Strangely most of his co-workers thought he was doing a good job. The paperwork was completed efficiently, the farm buildings had never been better equipped and the PCC meetings produced good plans. But deep down the man knew that things were not right. If all the farms were harvesting so little, how was the general population to be fed? He wasn't even sure that the farms were really in the farming business. After all wasn't food production supposed to be what farms were there for?

What would the Lord of the Manor say?

You don't have to talk long to a farmer before hearing something of the frustrations of the current economic climate for agriculture. For many, the only way to make ends meet is to diversify into areas which they would not consider farming at all – bed-and-breakfast, farm shops, camping sites and working museums. Those whose vocation and pride was in farming, producing food for the nation, can feel depressed and undervalued when farming activity is only kept alive because it is subsidized by Common Agricultural Policy grants and non-farming-related activity.

Whenever I get together with other rural clergy, similar frustrations emerge. As with the would-be-farmer of the parable, there seem to be so many things which must be done, many of which seem peripheral to the calling we had from the Lord of the Harvest. After the filling-in of faculty applications, the church fêtes, the round of services repeated in each village, and the PCC meetings, there is all too little time left for mission – which tends to be the thing that we do after we've fulfilled all our other obligations. As rural clergy, we tell ourselves that God's mission isn't only up to us. It is the job of the whole church. At the same time, we know that our priorities will be noted and our example followed. If others are to engage in mission, the priest's vocation is to lead the way.

Being on the working group which wrote *Mission-shaped Church*[1] brought it home to me again and again how easily I slip into thinking of mission and Church the wrong way round. Even now, I still find myself talking of mission in Church-centred ways, as if the point of mission were merely to make the Church grow or at least keep the Church alive: 'We need to bring more people in if the church is to have a future.' I guess it's because I still love the Church and old habits die hard. However, my priorities have changed. The mission of God is not only a higher calling than the maintenance of the Church. It is the very reason for which God brought the Church into being. If the Church in the countryside is to become a mission-shaped Church, it will be because we have remembered that we are servants in God's mission: 'It is not the Church of God that has a mission in the world, but the God of mission who has a church in the world.'[2]

Practically speaking, 'We need to stop starting with the Church'[3] and focus instead on God's mission. Instead of existing forms of church providing the limits and the shape that Christian mission can take, we need to discover the part of God's mission to which each Christian community is called and let God's mission limit and shape our churches.

To return to the comparison of the situation of rural clergy and farmers, the situation of rural clergy turns out to be significantly different from that of those involved in agriculture, despite the similar emotions involved. Food is not in short supply on our supermarket shelves. The agricultural industry has already fulfilled its main purpose – and we are dealing with a problem of surplus capacity. The Church of God, however, has not yet completely fulfilled its main purpose. There are plenty of people who have never tasted God's word. The Church's problem is not that we have produced too much fruit – but that the soil is stony, the predators and the weeds are prolific. When being fruitful is hard, it is easier to find some sort of sense of achievement by changing the focus away from harvest to keeping the 'farms' going.

What is the mission to which the Church is called?

In John 20.21, the risen Lord Jesus appears to his disciples, shows them the marks of the crucifixion and says:

> As the Father sent me, so I send you. Receive the Holy Spirit.

For the working group of the *Mission-shaped Church* report, these words were a constant reminder of the heart of Christian mission. Although, the passage is only directly quoted twice in the final document, in the shaping of our thoughts we returned to it again and again.

The remainder of this chapter looks at how three aspects of this passage inspire a more holistic perspective on mission, including rural mission. The passage has a trinitarian shape: mission comes from God the Father, through the Son in the power of the Spirit[4] – and its pattern is the pattern of the ministry of Jesus.

Mission comes from the Father, through the Son – starting with God

Jesus points to his Father as the initiator of his mission. For Christians the practical outworking of this order of things is that all mission starts with listening prayer. If it does not, it is not really mission as the New Testament understands it at all. Strategies dreamt up by PCCs to fill their churches can be full of great ideas – harvest suppers, *Alpha* courses, visiting schemes, carols round the tree – but the point is lost if they are not ideas from the mind of the Father. Maybe this is insultingly obvious to some readers, but I have to confess it does not always appear obvious to me. Indeed, there are days in rural ministry when it seems naively idealistic.

In the presence of God

When I arrived in the Tas Valley benefice, I thought I would set aside 40 days for prayer and fasting. I would do only those other parts of the ministry of the rector that were absolutely essential. I soon found out that you can fill 48 hours of every day with activity which seems absolutely essential and urgent especially after a long interregnum. At the end of the process, I could hardly say that I'd spent 40 days in prayer and fasting – rather I'd begun my ministry with 40 days of slightly more prayer than usual. It was clear that for me, booking a day at the local retreat house would be an essential

strategy in resisting the many distractions from spending a
longer period in the presence of the Almighty.

Listening prayer is not only important for priests and individual lay people, it
is also something we need to do in community. There are particular
challenges in seeking the mind of God with listening prayer in the rural
church: rural churches are not, on the whole, 'gathered' congregations. People
do not join because of their teaching or theology or churchmanship – they
come because it is the church in their village. Priests, readers and other
church leaders in this situation become accustomed to being inclusive in
their approach. The congregation of a rural church is usually small and
involves people of a great range of approaches to their faith. It is usually a
strength in a rural minister to concentrate on doing the things which all can
agree on and work on together – and not to rock the boat. In becoming
used to avoiding the needlessly controversial, there is a temptation for
leaders not to insist on the things which are of the very essence of what it is
to be church. Disciplined, listening prayer to discover God's heart for mission
in each community is one of those things which must be non-negotiable.

For multi-parish benefices, the sheer logistics of leading several churches also
militate against corporate listening prayer. Some village churches in multi-
parish benefices do not want to work together or meet together too often.
How and where the prayer takes place may seem like a big decision in itself.
However, it is essential to start. It may not be something which very many
people will join the ministers in at first – but it must be the source of the
church's/churches' vision. Otherwise, we are acting as if the mission were
ours instead of God's.

'Revival is coming'

One of the most remarkable stories of rural mission begins with just two elderly sisters pouring their hearts out to God for their community in the village of Barvas on the Isle of Lewis in 1949.[5] As they prayed, God gave one of them a simple vision. In it, she could see the parish church filled with young people. It was a particularly striking picture because at the time, not a single teenager lived in the village. Undaunted, the sisters took the vision as a promise from God and told their minister, 'Revival is coming.' Somewhat bewildered he replied, 'What do you suggest I do?' 'What should you do?' they gasped. 'You should *pray* man! If you will gather your elders and pray at the other end of the village at least two nights a week, we will do the same here.' The prayer meetings continued for three long months – during which I imagine the minister wondered why he had ever been talked into such excessive amounts of prayer. Then came a night when an awareness of God's presence exploded into one of the prayer meetings. For four years, this conscious-ness of God became felt in the streets, in the shops, the pubs and homes of people in many of the Hebridean islands. Sometimes people would wake in the middle of the night and feel they had to make their peace with God and were drawn to church. Whole communities were transformed as the gospel was embraced.

Mission in the power of the Spirit

Small rural churches can sometimes feel that they are the poor relation compared to larger urban and suburban churches – musical excellence is often out of reach, buildings may not be very well equipped for contemporary worship or community needs, the critical mass of committed people may not be large enough to engage in some kinds of ministry. When I am feeling frustrated at lack of resources, I try to remember the shell-shocked disciples of John 20: as soon as Jesus has told the disciples that he is sending them, he immediately says, 'Receive the Holy Spirit.' Perhaps our awareness of weakness can be a good thing if it leads us to rely on this source of power.

Rural church members will sometimes be very wary of talk of the Holy Spirit. In my experience, this happens when they associate talk of the Spirit with waving hands in the air, bizarre manifestations and guitar-led, hard-to-sing choruses. These can be particularly embarrassing in a small congregation. However, rural church communities frequently experience the Holy Spirit bringing unity and enabling the church family to live in grace amid the different preferences of worship styles. The Holy Spirit gives 'power from on high' to make disciples (Luke 24.47-49) of people from many different backgrounds without imposing conformity, but 'opening our eyes to Christ and to our fellow humans in Christ and their cultural needs'.[6] The story of Pentecost models the mission of the Church, 'translating the message'[7] into every language, including the languages of culture.[8]

> Thanks to the outpouring and action of the Spirit, who draws
> gifts and talents into unity, all the peoples of the earth, when
> they enter the church, live a new Pentecost, professing in their
> own tongue the one faith in Jesus.[9]

The *Mission-shaped Church* report puts particular emphasis on the 'Spirit's eschatological ministry'[10] as the guarantee of God's final new creation:

> The Bible tells us over and over again that God intends to
> make all things new ... God's kingdom is where the blind see,
> the deaf hear and the lame dance for joy. It is a future in
> which justice comes for the poor, peace to the nations and all
> visions of race, culture and national identity disappear as we
> discover we are all family together and we worship our God
> forever.[11]

It is the Holy Spirit who pours God's love into our hearts so that a taste of this new creation is anticipated in the community of the Church today. One example of such a community is seen in the new church formed in Jerusalem immediately after Pentecost (Acts 2.43-47). They met and ate together frequently and shared whatever they had generously, filled with gratitude to God. A community filled with the Holy Spirit can celebrate without falling into hedonism; rejoice in the material world of God's creation without materialism; love each individual as infinitely precious, without falling into individualism. Producing love, joy, peace, patience, kindness, goodness, gentleness, faithfulness, self-control (Galatians 5.22-23), the Holy Spirit makes Christian communities more holistic and mission-shaped. A community filled with the Holy Spirit will be a place of healing and refuge for the hurting and desperate.

This ministry of the Spirit is a wonderful reminder to me as a rural minister that however few material resources are available to us, small churches are not the poor relation in what really matters. If the Holy Spirit calls us to translate the gospel message afresh in each new cultural context, then rural churches are uniquely placed to do this in the countryside. We are the communities where, by God's grace, rural dwellers may see and hear the reality of Jesus.

The pattern of Jesus' mission – 1. Incarnation

'As the Father sent me, so I send you,' says Jesus. Therefore, the question of *how* the Father sent Jesus is key. The Incarnation is unique in the sense that only God can take human nature for the salvation of his creation. However, it is also a pattern for Jesus' disciples. The Father sent Jesus to become a human being – 'one of us': it follows that Christian disciples in every age are to become like those to whom we are sent. The Christian Church is to share the lives, the hopes and fears, pains and joys, the culture and language of the people to whom God has sent it. However, following the pattern of Christ's incarnation does not mean a church takes on all aspects of any culture uncritically: 'A truly incarnational church, is one that imitates ... both Christ's loving identification with his culture and his costly countercultural stance within it.'[12]

In the Gospels, we see Jesus engaging fully in the prevailing culture of first-century Palestine and yet challenging it to its core with the values of God's kingdom. He worships in the synagogue on the Sabbath – but also heals on that day – for God's day cannot be a day without healing. He travels around like other contemporary rabbis but, unlike many others, holds up those on the edges of society as signs of God's grace – children, Samaritans, women and the disabled get special attention.

I particularly love the way the apostle Paul sought to apply what missiologists call 'the incarnational principle'[13] in his own ministry, identifying with both Jew and Gentile:

> To the Jews I became as a Jew, in order to win Jews. To those under the law I became as one under the law (though I myself am not under the law) so that I might win those under the law. To those outside the law I became as one outside the law (though I am not free from God's law but am under Christ's law) so that I might win those outside the law. To the weak I became weak, so that I might win the weak. I have become all things to all people, that I might by all means save some. I do it all for the sake of the gospel, so that I may share its blessings. (1 Corinthians 9.20-23, NRSV)

Paul saw God as already working among all peoples and as having created the nations of the earth in order that they may seek after him (Acts 17.23-28). He proclaimed a God who even pagan Athenians already worshipped unknowingly and in whom they 'lived and moved and had their being.' The implication is that we do not approach the task of mission as if to an utterly Godless world. Rather, we expect to find among every group of people, every culture, some echoes of God, some knowledge of God because he made us in his image. This idea is expressed beautifully by the second-century writer Justin Martyr. God created the world through his Word (Christ) and therefore seeds of the Word are to be found in all human thought although not yet fully known:

> All those writers were able through the seed of the Word implanted in them to see reality darkly. For it is one thing to have the seed of a thing and to imitate it up to one's capacity; far different is the thing itself, shared and imitated in virtue of its own grace.[14]

Christians proclaiming the gospel expect to learn as well as to give, so that as people from different cultures come to Christ their cultures change and enrich the existing church culture.[15]

In rural England as elsewhere, this incarnational principle means that church communities need to listen, understand and fully enter into the complex cultural reality of the area or network of people to which God has called them. Therefore churches that serve rural areas will end up looking different from urban or suburban ones.

Parish churches in the countryside are naturally drawn to an incarnational approach in that they are inheritors of a tradition that has sought to build on people's innate spirituality rather than dismiss it as inadequate or super-stitious. For example, the celebration of harvest and rogation can be seen as the churches' attempts to respond incarnationally to the deep awareness of the natural world often found in those who work on the land. However, rural culture is changing. The declining attendance at such services[16] partly reflects the fact that fewer rural dwellers are involved in farming today. To follow the pattern of Christ's incarnation, Christian communities will need to learn to enter into the newer cultural realities emerging in rural England.

No parish church can speak equally clearly within every culture found in rural areas. We might ask who is going to be most at home – a member of the WI or a teenager; the local chippy or a retired army colonel? For many people within parish churches, the love and worship they find there helps them to see the gospel in action. For them, the Church has come alongside them like Jesus in the Incarnation. But for others in today's society there is a credibility gap. In a quick-fix, highly consumerized culture, for many people the idea of going to a medieval building to sing to an organ, read some prayers and listen to a talk based on the text of an ancient book does not appear as if it would help them discover the meaning of the universe, never mind have any bearing on everyday struggles with work, debts, addictions or relationships. Reaching these people will require following the pattern of the Incarnation, setting aside our preferences to live the gospel within a different culture.

The pattern of Jesus' mission – 2. Dying to live

In John chapter 20, the risen Jesus shows his disciples his hands and side and tells them, 'Peace be with you. As the Father sent me, so I send you.' It seems to me that his scars are an all too graphic visual aid for what being sent by the Father has meant for Jesus: in dying, he took servanthood to the limit and in rising was transformed.

Christians know this is what brings us forgiveness and a fresh start. However, I am learning in my own life and ministry that this isn't just about accepting this as the story of our salvation – but also about entering into it. There is a very practical side to 'taking up our cross' and experiencing the power of Christ's resurrection (Philippians 3.10-11). In the baptism service, we talk of this as 'dying to sin that we might live his risen life'.[17]

If dying to live is normative for every aspect of the obedient Christian life, mission is naturally no exception. A Church shaped for mission will be one shaped for the sake of those to whom it is sent in mission, not one shaped to meet the needs of its own members:

> The Church is most true to itself when it gives itself up, in current cultural form, to be reformed among those who do not know God's son. In each new context, the Church must die to live.[18]

One biblical image used in the *Mission-shaped Church* report to explore the significance of 'dying to live' in mission is that of the planted seed.[19] In John 12, Jesus is responding to the fact that Gentiles are seeking him out. He says, 'Unless a grain of wheat falls into the earth and dies, it remains just a single grain; but if it dies, it bears much fruit' (John 12.24): Jesus is speaking of his own imminent death as the planting of a seed. Although it is the end of the seed in one sense, it is also the beginning to a whole new life. Jesus' death and resurrection will bring to fruition all that he has worked for and enable the gospel to be planted among the Gentiles in a new way. Jesus continues by applying this 'dying to live' principle to all who follow him: 'If you love your life, you will lose it. If you give it up in this world, you will be given eternal life' (John 12.25).

The image of planting a seed is particularly relevant to the dynamic of starting a brand new church – church planting or setting up some mission initiatives. The seed stands for the missionary team, seeking to live out the gospel in word and deed. They come from some particular sending church with its own culture. They have to be willing to set aside those preferences and customs, which seem normal and natural to them, in order to immerse themselves in new cultural soil. They have to 'die' to the sort of church they have come from – otherwise they may impose that on the people with whom they are seeking to share the gospel. This cannot ever be other than painful – for we all would be more comfortable in a church shaped to fit us.

'Dying to live' means it is those who consider themselves mature in faith that make the sacrifices, not those who are just beginning to explore the Christian faith. The missionary team give up their preferences. The aim must be for a cultural grouping to create church within their own culture – so that others like them can see and hear the reality of Jesus authentically lived in their own cultural terms. In the Prologue, we saw how the congregation at Swainsthorpe made the sacrifice of changing one service a month from their preferred style in order to reach out to local families. Another sacrifice is seen in the story of the church in the Norfolk village of Ashill:

story story story story

The pain of parting[20]

Over a period of about ten years the churches at Ashill and Saham Toney (two Norfolk villages, total population about 3,000) had experienced growth through charismatic renewal. They began to be more widely missionary through *Alpha* courses, visiting Wayland prison and the starting of 'Living Water' – a four-day Christian festival on the Norfolk Showground.

A large number of young families attended the church of St Nicholas, Ashill, and they along with most of the PCC wanted to remove some of the pews to allow more flexible use of the worship space. However, this met with strong resistance from some villagers and worshippers and after much prayer and heart-searching, the rector, the Revd Martin Down started up a new congregation, 'The Fountain of Life', in the village hall. The separation of the two different groups within the parish was a real bereavement on both sides. For some of those who joined the new congregation, St Nicholas church building was where generations of their family had been christened, married and buried. For both the traditional congregation and the new one there were close friends or family members in the other expression of church. Yet those who left the parish church to found the new congregation did not feel they were being pushed out. Rather, that this was their calling, to set up a new church and to watch God bless both churches.

Ten years on, after more sacrifices and difficult times for many of the people involved, it is clear that the two churches are called to different aspects of God's mission. St Nicholas, Ashill, has a good parish-based ministry. The Fountain of Life now has a separate identity as a growing network church serving a wide area. It is a registered charity and a Missionary Congregation of the Church of England currently seeking official status under the new pastoral measure. At the time of writing the average congregation is 150. They have purchased their own building and paid for the adaptation out of personal giving. The worship area will seat 200 people and is fully equipped with modern technology. There is a church office, meeting rooms, kitchen and counselling rooms.

A new heart for mission has emerged. Martin having retired, the new church leader is Stephen Mawditt, formerly Martin's curate. He meets regularly with the area bishop and they seek to develop ways of mission to parts of the community that are hard for parish churches to reach.

'Dying to live' does not only speak of making sacrifices for the sake of the kingdom. It also speaks of God's grace, which brings fresh life out of death, error and failure:

On the edge

When I was a curate in rural Worcestershire, my husband and I ran a small youth group who called themselves 'On the Edge'. It was an appropriately named group, always struggling for a sustainable core of young people, and eventually the group 'fell off the edge' and was no more. We were deeply disappointed and hurt – what had we done wrong? But the experience drove us to prayer and, giving up the wish for a benefice-based youth group, to co-operation with others. A new group was begun based on the catchment area of the secondary school in the parish, and leaders came from three rural benefices. This group flourished and continued to grow and develop with new leaders after we moved on. Today, it involves over 20 young people in peer-led cells and could be considered as a fresh expression of church in its own right.

From rural church-shaped mission to rural mission-shaped church

Often, in talking about mission in the past, I have started with mission projects: an *Alpha* course, an old peoples' luncheon club, a Christian library or the visit of an evangelistic preacher. However, in John 20, the mention of particular projects is notably absent. 'As the Father sent me, so I send (*missio*)[21] you.' It is a striking reminder to me that God's mission is not about doing certain isolated projects as if we could complete a certain amount and then get on with the rest of our non-missionary lives. If Jesus' mission was the whole life God sent him to live, ours is joining our whole lives to his.

In this chapter, we have seen that a mission-shaped church in any context recognizes that mission is not an add-on activity: rather, it is the reason the Church exists; Church is born through mission. This mission always comes from God the Father, through the Son in the power of the Spirit [22] – and its pattern is the pattern of the ministry of Jesus in his incarnation and 'dying to live'. The incarnational principle means that mission-shaped churches in the countryside can only be those who enter into their rural context. Therefore the next chapter is about listening to rural culture.

2 Listening to rural culture

There's more than one rural England

story
story
story
story

When I arrived in 1996 as the new curate in the then united benefice of Martey, Wichenford, Broadwas, Cotheridge and Knightwick with Doddenham, I soon learned that I had entered another world from that of my suburban upbringing. In each village, one member of the congregation was assigned to spend a day showing me round and introducing me to local people. In Knightwick, this task fell to Helen Walker (the younger), the wife of one of the churchwardens. I soon discovered that nearly every house we visited was owned by the Walker family or had previously been owned by them. Those who lived there were employees of the Walker estate or had previously been so. The Walker clan was extensive – and when Mrs Walker (Helen's mother-in-law) offered to draw up a family tree for me, this was indeed a useful resource in understanding the parish. Peter was the fifth generation continuous warden in the parish, with his great-great-grandfather being first 'elected' in 1850. Another of his great-grandfathers had been rector of the parish.

In this tiny parish, the remains of a benign feudalism still survived – and the Walker family considered it their responsibility to care for the church. Miss Mary (Peter's aunt) played the organ and cared for the little chapel of ease adjacent to her home at the Old Rectory. Peter and Helen bedecked the chancel with a magnificent arch of fresh hops each year and hosted the Harvest Supper – lamb stew with a lamb from the farm of another Walker slaughtered specially for the occasion and plenty of pies made from locally grown apples.

In 1996, the farm door was always open – and there was always someone around to chat over coffee and to defend me from 'Christmas', one of the geese, that was too aggressive for my liking. But things move on. By 2000, Helen was working outside the farm full time as a nurse – and today the farm itself has been sold, albeit to some Walker cousins. Peter is warden of a parish, now united with two more villages, and has begun also working with a group called 'Go West' which was set up post Foot and Mouth by the Agricultural Chaplaincy to promote rural regeneration through tourism, with the history of the church and church buildings at its root. His sons look unlikely to succeed him as churchwarden.

My memories of Knightwick epitomize for me much that I think of as 'rural life', but in reality rural England is very diverse and it is hard to generalize about the rural environment and culture. There is a temptation to emphasize the parts of rural life that fit in with an idyllic fantasy.

Farmed countryside is people's traditional picture of rural England – a landscape of fields and farm buildings dotted with villages, hamlets, woodlands and open space.[1]

To understand the countryside as it really is in all its diversity is important because engaging in mission starts with listening. Rural churches too are called to show the gospel incarnate, in all the culture(s) of today's countryside.

The shape of different rural communities is very much affected by the agriculture that has historically taken place there, as well as proximity to other centres of population and work and factors to do with population shifts and tourism. Although the changes that have taken place at the farm at Knightwick during the last decade mirror many of the changes taking place right across rural Britain, these do take a quite different form, say, in Norfolk, where agriculture tends to be dominated by arable rather than mixed farming and the family farm is rarer.

There is no widely accepted simple definition of what constitutes 'rural', although there is agreement that the term describes an area with settlements of less than ten thousand inhabitants. From 2004, new definitions of rural and urban, developed through the collaboration of five government organizations,[2] have been used in government publications. These use three measurement criteria to classify hectare grid squares:

1. settlement form (dispersed dwellings, hamlet, village, small town, urban fringe, urban)

2. sparsity or remoteness

3. function (the number and type of commercial addresses)

A clearly rural area would be remote or sparsely populated with hamlets, villages or a small town, and where the land is dominated by agriculture. However, within areas classified as rural, there are still many variations. There can be as much difference between a rural community of a dozen households and one of 1,000 as there is between one of 1,000 and a suburban environment.

In this book, examples of mission-shaped churches are included from a broad variety of rural environments. However, it is written with a special eye to the particular issues in ministry and mission in smaller centres of population (under 2,000) where churches may be grouped in multi-parish benefices or share a priest and where there are less community amenities.

Distinctives of rural life and cultural change

Agriculture and environment

In popular imagination rural life is centred around the land and around farming as a way of life. In reality, less than 2 per cent of the UK population is employed in agriculture, fisheries and forestry[3] and many rural dwellers may not know a single person engaged in work in these areas. This is particularly true in the south and east where there are larger arable farms although here there may be more flexible use of hired labour. In the north and west, farms are smaller, more mixed and more dependent upon family labour.

Farmers have often become socially isolated as farming has become less labour intensive. As one rural bishop recently commented in a newspaper article:

> There is a division between rural dwellers and farmers, sometimes because of the nature of farming they tend to, in some instances, disassociate themselves from society. Also due to the nature of their work they are isolated from the community because of their long hours.[4]

Although those involved with farming are in a minority, they occupy a special place in the mission context of the countryside. This is partly because in our society they have been marginalized, and hence the Church is especially called to hear their voice. This has been particularly important in the recent Foot and Mouth epidemic and before that in the Beef Crisis. However, it has been a time of substantial and unsettling change even without these catastrophes. Farm gate prices have been down year on year. Tens of thousands of people are leaving full time employment in farming every year and over a quarter of farms no longer pass on to sons or daughters when the present farmer retires.

Secondly, the farming community often still embodies values which much of the rest of society has lost. Among their number are often the people with the deepest roots in a particular locality who have cared for the same land for generations. They may frequently have a sense of great wonder at creation and be committed to ideals of stewardship of the land for future generations.

Holding these two things together is part of the great challenge to farmers as they face choices about diversification. While farmers themselves often feel isolated and powerless, government figures suggest that 75 per cent of countryside is held for agricultural use – and farmers hold the key to the future of our rural landscape. The Countryside Agency predicts significant change for farming, shaped by forces outside the control of farmers:

- environmental anxiety and responsibility and the sustainability ideal in an uneasy alliance with bio and information technologies;

- individualism, consumerism and choice;

- universalism and globalization versus polarization and tribalism;
- heritage and nostalgia.

> Over the next 20 years farming will remain the spine of much
> of the countryside, but not farming as we have known it.
> There will be two big stories: new economic opportunities for
> farming and the diversification of land management . . . A twin-
> track pattern of agriculture will therefore emerge; on the one
> hand highly capitalized, highly mechanized, highly specialized,
> large scale, often orientated to world markets; on the other
> hand smaller-scale, high value-added, and focused on local and
> niche markets.[5]

Tourism

When most people think of the countryside, it is not agriculture or food
production which comes to mind in the first instance. Rather, the
countryside is where urban dwellers go to 'get away from it all'. According to
the 2002–3 Great Britain Day Visits Survey, the total number of leisure day
visits to rural areas in England was 1.3 billion for the year.[6] Many of these
visits will be to particularly famous beauty spots, but it remains true that
walking (mainly in the countryside) is the most popular leisure activity in
Britain. The 2001 Foot and Mouth crisis made clear for the first time how
significant a factor tourism has become in the rural economy. Government
figures for 2002 estimated that agriculture contributes £7.1 billion and
countryside day trips £9 billion to the UK economy.[7]

For rural dwellers, tourism is a mixed blessing. Where farming is at the
margins of economic viability, access over land can cause additional difficulties
for the farmer – especially if the correct rights of way are not observed. In
areas of high tourist activity, the visitors themselves can pose a risk to the
natural environment they came to admire. On the other hand, tourists
spend money and hence contribute to the local economy. Without tourists,
many a local shop, pub or train service would not be economically viable.
However, the average spend of £7.30 per visit[8] does not compare favourably
with the average spend of a leisure visitor to an urban area (£15.30) or
seaside (£12.60).

Among the tourists themselves, the draw to the countryside has a lot to do with 'retreat, revival, re-creation and risk' which, as John Saxbee has pointed out, are fundamentally theological and spiritual ideas.[9] Where a small rural church or chapel is left open, a glance through the visitors' book or prayer requests board speaks volumes about visitors' search for peace, and gratitude for the beauty and tranquillity of the countryside.

Population shift

Migration has changed the face of the countryside: '70% of people who live in rural communities today are first-generation villagers who either moved there in their life-time or are the first in their family to be born in that situation.'[10] Migration from urban to rural areas is now running at four times the migration from the north of the country to the south.[11] Indigenous rural dwellers are now in the minority.

Many of these urban incomers seek out a home in the countryside with similar ideas to the tourist – the countryside will offer them a place of retreat and recreation. Commuters seek an attractive place to live when not at work. Retired people seek the peace and beauty of the surroundings. There are problems for the rural community in these reasons for buying properties in the countryside. While the countryside is seen as a retreat, it is not seen as the main focus of life. Commuters may have little time or energy after long daily journeys to the city to invest in village activities. Those who have a 'second home' in the countryside cannot possibly contribute to community life in the way that a household permanently resident and investing their whole lives in the area did in the past. Even among those who retire to the countryside, a substantial proportion spend long periods away from home on holidays or with family and friends outside the area. Hence, an increase in housing stock has not prevented a weakening of community life. As the concept of the rural idyll attracts wealthier urban dwellers to the countryside, house prices are driven up and young adults who have grown up and feel they belong in a particular rural community often cannot afford to live there except by remaining in the parental home.

However, it is not true that there are few young people in the countryside. Under 16s account for 18.1 per cent of the population (close to the urban figure of 18.7 per cent). In the year to mid 2002, 34.1 per cent of migrants to the countryside were under 15 and 48.5 per cent were adults between the ages of 25 and 44.[12] This may be because people in this age group consider the countryside to be a safer place to raise children. The 16–24 age range is the only one in which more people migrated to urban districts than to rural. Even though many adults with young families commute long distances to work, their children's involvement at a local school is likely to pull them into the social fabric of the area

Social capital

Social capital describes the level of reciprocal relationships and trustworthy networks which exist within a particular locality or community. A strong sense of community has traditionally been the stuff of the countryside. Rural communities are still regarded as more vibrant and the idea of the close-knit village where everyone knows everyone else is important as a memory and a cherished ideal. Nevertheless, in most places it no longer describes the present reality. Mark Rylands, missioner in Devon, talks of how this sad change is typified by the collapse of an old wattle and daub house in the rural village of Doulton. When it happened, nobody knew who to contact, for the owners lived away and their neighbours in the village had had no contact with them.

The Countryside Report 2003 noted much more social contact and civic engagement in rural than in urban areas. However, increased mobility has led to a weakening of the focal meeting places. Shops and post offices are closing because of competition with supermarkets and the better facilities of cities. There are fewer than 12,000 rural shops left in Britain and the number reduces by an estimated 300 every year. Country pubs in England are shutting at a rate of six a week.[13]

In addition, the population shift from urban to rural has contributed to social fragmentation and this is set to continue. Some incomers arrive with unrealistic expectations – of peace and quiet or a slower pace of life. In their own desire to retreat from industrialization, they do not always recognize that in the countryside they are living in a working environment under threat. Stories abound of urban incomers who object to the smells and noises of the farm and rural business. To those who have lived in the countryside longer, it can feel that an invasion of articulate powerful people with fantasies about the countryside is misinforming policies from politicians and planners. Another point of tension is that people have sometimes arrived in the countryside with an imagined view of the rural ideal and expect locals to conform to it – attempts to 'create community' by newcomers may not go down too well with those whose understanding of 'community' is rather different.

The State of the Countryside 2020 report predicts:

> Conflicts will become more numerous as the rural population grows and differences will be resolved on the (utilitarian) basis of what works for most people rather than by appeal to any shared ideal about the countryside. Pragmatism also reflects and reinforces post-modern values in society at large, as people increasingly live mosaic lives jumping from one network, subculture and system to another . . . The triumph of pragmatism may mean there is no court of values to which the weak can appeal. The lack of an overarching vision . . . may therefore enable 'what works best' to become 'what works best for the strongest group'.[14]

In many rural villages, there used to be one recognizable shared culture for that community in living memory. The churches were a central part of that culture. Among older villagers and particularly within the churches there is often a sense of nostalgia for that time and even sometimes denial that those times will never return. Today, rural areas are full of people who belong to different 'networks' and subcultures. Farmers are a good example of a network culture with common experiences and meetings around livestock markets or farmers' markets. Other networks are focused on local schools or on places of work and leisure way beyond the parish boundaries. Different networks present in the countryside have different values and it may be difficult for each small parish church to respond effectively to this diversity.

National trends in the rural context

A British Rip Van Winkle, falling asleep in the 1970s and waking up just 30 years later would be deeply aware of speaking to people from a quite different culture to his own. Our national culture has been changing faster than ever before in history.

Since the publication of the *Mission-shaped Church* report, I have been talking with deanery synods in the rural Diocese of Norwich about some key changes outlined in the report: greater mobility; changes in employment; divorce and changes in family life, the weakening of neighbourhoods; the power of networks, consumerism, the death of Christendom. I thought that deeply committed, often conservative, rural Christians might perceive these societal changes as less marked in rural than in urban areas. What I have discovered in conversation is that these particular changes are not only valid for rural areas but their impact has been in many ways more acute. This is partly because many of these trends lead directly away from the stereotype of the 'rural idyll' which is still a dream of many rural dwellers. It is also because the changes have happened relatively quickly with little time for community life to adapt. Finally, with smaller geographical communities, some changes have led to the loss of critical mass for the previous quality of village community life to continue.

Some of their observations on these key societal changes are noted below:

- *Greater mobility* – Incomers have moved further away from family for the rural lifestyle and therefore spend more 'free time' travelling to see friends and relations living at a distance with consequent impact on local weekend activities in the village.

- *Employment changes* – With more women working during the week as well as men, the army of younger women who used to run community activities are no longer available and much of the fabric of village life is held together only by the older generation.

- *Divorce and changes in family life* – Divorce rates have increased and village children are often away at weekends visiting another parent.

- *Weakening neighbourhoods* –The sense of obligation to 'our village' has weakened. People see less of neighbours than 30 years ago and community organizations of all kinds are weaker.

- *The power of networks* – Community is often formed around networks of choice – where we work, the pub we frequent, the gym, the school, the Internet chat-room. Many people are part of a range of networks – the less mobile and the poor may not be part of any network at all and are the big losers in the decline of neighbour-hood-based community.

- *A consumer culture* – Shopping has become a favourite national pastime and draws people out of the village to the town. Not only that, consumerist values affect the way we respond to ideas too. If we don't agree with what someone says, we might say, 'I don't buy that.' A sense of duty to the village and village church has declined and been replaced by a belief in personal choice. Religion and values may be chosen by each individual as if at the 'pick-and-mix' counter at the supermarket.

- *The death of Christendom* – When *Faith in the Countryside* was published in 1990, the authors could say, 'In rural areas, it is often wise to avoid too clear a distinction between the Christian life as lived in the Church and the Christian life as lived in society.'[15] Today, many in rural areas would feel that an unwarranted assumption was being made if they were assumed to regard themselves as Christian without their claiming the title by some sort of association with the church. Christianity is no longer a universally accepted authority – merely as one among many competing lifestyles and truth claims which may be chosen by the individual. It used to be said that whereas in the town, people belonged to a church, in the countryside, the church belonged to the people. Today, while such a sense of ownership is still greater than in urban areas, many rural dwellers would see the affairs of the local church as none of their concern.

Features of the rural church

Listening and seeking to understand a context is only a first step in planting or becoming a mission-shaped church. Missionaries talk about 'double listening'. This usually refers to listening to our own church tradition as well as the missionary context.[16] This is important because of the human tendency to assume that the tradition of one's own church is simply the proper way to do things. Here are a few of the features of most Anglican rural churches which people like myself tend to take for granted:

- Sunday services

- hymn singing

- small congregations

- a mixture of ages or more older people

- teaching mainly through sermons

- worship based strongly on the written word

- part of a multi-parish benefice

- clergy

- historic church building.

It is important consciously to take a step back from the things we take for granted to do a third form of listening – listening to God to discern how mission and church should develop in response to the particular cultural context. Many of the 'normal' ways of being church may be part of the answer and may embody essential gospel values – others will look a bit strange and unnecessary when we start to look from the point of view of the people to whom we feel God is sending us. The report advises, 'Make sure the mission-questions drive the church-answers, not vice versa.'[17]

Towards a rural mission-shaped church

Listening is to be followed by the response of entering into the pattern of Christ's incarnation – to become like those to whom we are sent. Churches are to share the lives, the hopes and fears, pains and joys, the culture and language of the people to whom God has sent them. To be faithful in mission, churches must enter into the pattern of dying to live – giving up the preferences of members to identify with those to whom he sends us; engaging in the culture around us while proclaiming the values of the kingdom within it; serving to the end and being transformed by God's grace.

Mission-shaped churches can be old or new, but it would be expected that their most distinctive current features would be those that have developed in response to the cultures in which they engage in mission. In the next chapter we look at inculturation – as the process by which the gospel penetrates to the heart of culture. We will see examples of how churches old and new are engaging in inculturation in response to the very important developments in rural culture outlined in this chapter.

3 Engaging with rural culture

Gardening on the wild side

Our rectory is set in the middle of a large and unkempt garden. It's a great place for our young son to play hide and seek with his friends and he'll also join me from time to time in a spot of gardening. We've cultivated lettuces, tomatoes and strawberries with some success. The beans and pumpkin seedlings sadly got eaten by wild rabbits. We've also benefited from the efforts of past generations of gardeners with blackcurrants and apples but the plum tree is busy competing with a self-seeded elder and seems to have given up on fruit. About twice a week, I look out on the garden and sigh and think how much the messy garden is like my own ministry.

The patch is too large for me. There is never enough time to do what needs to be done. I do a bit of pruning, a bit of planting, watering and weeding – and it makes some difference. However, it's not mainly down to me – the ground is amazingly fertile and I have to credit God for everything growing so amazingly. Of course, not all things grow equally well, some things self-seed and flourish with no encouragement whatsoever. Some are well established and continue with a minimum of attention. Others I have simply put in the wrong place so that they wither despite my best efforts.

The cultural soil in the benefice in which I minister is all important in determining what happens when a seed of the gospel is planted. Some churches are strong and steady like well-established trees. Some are threatened by developments in wider society like the plum tree. Some are fragile seedlings and I wait with excitement to see what will grow. This vital interaction between Church, gospel and culture is described by the process of inculturation.

This chapter falls into two parts. The first part describes the process of inculturation – and looks at its principles as they relate both to church-planting and to the ongoing transformation of existing churches. The second part looks at examples of inculturation in practice as churches old and new engage with the distinctive aspects of rural culture described in Chapter 2.

The process of inculturation

What is inculturation?

'Inculturation' is a term, used in the *Mission-shaped Church* report, which comes out of the churches' experience in cross-cultural mission abroad. It is essentially another term for the process of evangelization, but it draws attention to the need for the gospel to penetrate to the heart of a culture in the process.[1]

Culture is an essential part of being human. People find it difficult to describe their own culture because it is the air that they breathe. It involves the customs, symbols and values that they take for granted. As Lesslie Newbigin has said, 'If you want to find out about water, don't ask a fish.' We often don't recognize the importance of culture until we come across someone living in a different one from our own.

A missionary travelling abroad to a foreign culture would not go with a fixed idea of what the Church should look like. Rather, he or she would go to listen and to learn how the gospel is revealed in that culture. The process of inculturation can be likened to a conversation between the Church (engaging in mission and expressing the gospel in terms of its own culture) and the different culture within which the gospel is being shared. Into this conversation, breaks a third voice, the voice of God himself, bringing the gospel challenge and transformation to both conversation partners.

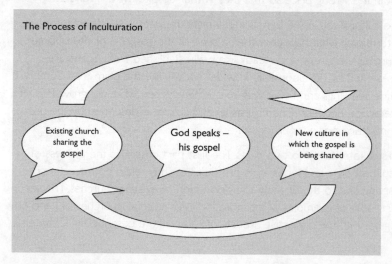

The Process of Inculturation

Existing church sharing the gospel

God speaks – his gospel

New culture in which the gospel is being shared

The *Mission-shaped Church* report reminded us that this is not only a conversation for mission abroad. In our fast changing culture, we too must engage in this conversation, listening to the voice of God, the voice of the existing Church and the voices living in the various non-churched cultures and subcultures of our society. This is not a merely pragmatic decision – adapting to cultural change because we must. It is a theological decision, based on the pattern of God's own mission. The theological basis of inculturation is to be found in the work of Father, Son and Holy Spirit in creation, redemption and the anticipation of God's new creation.[2]

Inculturation and church planting

Church planting is a process by which a seed of the life and message of Jesus embodied by a community of Christians is immersed for mission reasons in a particular cultural or geographic context. The intended consequence is that it roots there, coming to life as a new indigenous body of Christian disciples well suited to continue in mission.

The terms 'church planting' and 'inculturation' describe the same process. The only difference is that church planting refers only to the part of the process when a new church is begun. There are three stages in inculturation:[3]

1. **Translation** – Through double listening the missionary community seeks to adapt their initial presentation of the gospel to communicate it in a new cultural setting.

2. **Assimilation** – The missionary community and people belonging to the new cultural setting assimilate something of each other's cultures within a new Church.

3. **Transformation/ inculturation proper** – There is an ongoing process of critical exchange between the Church and the culture in which it is set. In this exchange, the Church seeks to understand what it means to live by gospel values in this cultural setting. This is a 'dying to live' process, involving sacrifice on the part of the Church leading to ongoing transformation both within the Church and the wider society.

While the first stage of inculturation is an activity of the church planter, the second and third stages are ongoing and are essential to any mission-shaped church. You don't need to have heard the term 'inculturation' in order to be practising it. Without this natural ongoing process of critical exchange between a church community and the wider culture in which it is set, a church will either become a cultural ghetto, inaccessible to the nonchurched, or it will lose its faithfulness to those gospel values which are countercultural in its setting.

Inculturation and the parish church

Saxlingham

The village of Saxlingham in the benefice where I am the Team Rector has two thriving churches. There is the non-denominational chapel which attracts people from a wide area and does some effective children's ministry, and there is the parish church: St Mary's, Saxlingham, is in the heart of its community, a village of under 700 people. Members of the church are involved in the village Players, the Gardening Club, the school governors and the parish council. Some of the church members run the 'Monday Mardle',[4] a social club for elderly people, in the church room. The church fête is one of the highlights of the village year. The Sunday congregation meets in a picturesque building in the centre of the village and is steadily growing. At the time of writing forty to fifty people attend worship – led with a light touch by my colleague Phil Wood, their team vicar. The service is modern language but has a traditional feel and the hymn singing is ably led by a small but enthusiastic robed choir.

Why is this simple traditional village church formula working so well? Part of the answer is given by Bob Jackson when he says, 'Churches do not need sophisticated resources to grow. They need high quality relationships.'[5] St Mary's Church, Saxlingham, loves and supports the members of their congregation and their sizable fringe in the rest of the village. It is also true to say that they have, possibly without realizing it, engaged in inculturation of the gospel for a particular cultural grouping which happens to be dominant in their village and the surrounding area. This group is

- well educated/middle class;

- mainly born before 1960;

- already knowledgeable of church from childhood onwards which makes the style of worship and customs of the church feel comfortable and familiar;

- able and wishing to spend social time within the village community.

This cultural grouping would applaud Anthony Russell in his words, 'In every generation, the pastoral strategy of the rural church has been founded on the consecrated building and the ordained clergyman; on the holy place and the sacred person.'[6] For them, the traditional patterns of the parish church still make complete sense and the residence of an able part-time vicar within the parish makes pastoral and worship expectations easier to fulfil than in many smaller villages within the multi-parish benefice.

Anecdotal evidence would suggest that Saxlingham is not untypical of many rural churches. Those who are able to provide good quality Sunday schools and family services are also reasonably successful in attracting some younger people.

The Times' religious affairs correspondent who wrote in 1985, 'The Church of England faces extinction in the countryside in the next twenty years'[7] has been proved wrong – partly due to the resilience of small churches and partly due to the population shift towards rural areas. However, the profile of those who typically attend rural congregations does suggest that the next forty years may be another story. The kinds of people who are most attracted to rural congregations are declining in numbers as years go by. The organization Christian Research predicts that on present trends, about 2,000 rural churches would be closed by 2020, and virtually all rural churches would be gone by 2040 by which time church attendance would be down to 2 per cent of the population.[8]

Even if these predictions of decline also prove to be overly pessimistic, new forms of church will still be needed alongside the inherited model. This is because the Christian call is not to fill church buildings but to enter into every culture in order to preach the gospel – to give to all the opportunity to see and hear the reality of Jesus. For example, there are minority groups within Saxlingham for whom St Mary's form of church is not attractive – for example the young and the previously nonchurched. This is not a criticism of the traditional parish church, so much as a recognition that the countryside is peopled by a variety of groupings and subcultures and it is not possible to meet each 'where they are' through a single expression of church.

St Mary's, Saxlingham, has to work with other churches and fresh expressions of church in seeking to meet the full spectrum of spiritual needs of those in the parish. In doing this, we are seeking to follow the example of the earliest apostles who were not content with founding a new Christian community among the Jews. They knew that God wanted to reach every people group in the world and sent Paul and others to undertake this mission. We too need to grow new forms alongside the old.

> We need to assess the old and value where and for whom it works, while alongside that, investing in, creating and nurturing a diversity of the new. [9]

Investing in, creating and nurturing a diversity of the new

In his book, *Hope for the Church*, Bob Jackson suggests that the greatest failure of the Church of England's 'gardening' in the twentieth century stemmed from a fundamental horticultural mistake. 'We treated our churches as if they were all oak trees – able to grow to any size and live virtually for ever. One plant could fill the whole parish garden more or less permanently.' [10] Here is the model of the parish church, stable and solid down the ages. However, gardens do not only contain oak trees and in a fast moving culture like our own, they might not be the only plant to be cultivating. Suppose that we were to plant something more like primroses: they have a limited, vigorous individual life, and they grow and spread to fill the ground by division into large numbers of individual plants. The God-given capacity of the Church to grow does not lie only in the Church's growth hormones but also in reproduction.

Rural church planting is typically the planting of primroses, rather than oaks. The term used by the *Mission-shaped Church* report is 'fresh expressions of church'. A fresh expression of church is typically small and fragile, based on networks of relationships rather than a geographical location and working to complement the parish churches by reaching out to those to whom parish churches are less well placed to minister. Many fresh expressions of church start under the auspices of a PCC but they are more than an additional activity of the parish church or stepping-stone for people to come to the usual Sunday services. A fresh expression of church is or has the potential to become fully church for those who take part.

In less densely populated areas, it often makes sense for a fresh expression of church to be planted to reach networks of people over a larger geographical area than the single parish. Sometimes the mission itself demands this, as with a youth congregation, working across all the parishes of a high school's catchment area. Sometimes it is required by the scarcity of leadership. Few church planters are placed in rural parishes. In a multi-parish benefice, clergy and readers will be already ministering in half a dozen or more separate congregations and could not sustain new initiatives in each parish. Since church planting in rural areas is, almost always, growing a new expression of church alongside the old, sensitivity is particularly needed towards the relationship between fresh expressions of church and small parish churches that could see fresh expressions as 'competition'. However, small congregations may welcome a fresh expression of church if it serves a clearly different part of the community, releasing the congregation from the pressure to change a dearly held worship style or to attempt the impossible task of meeting the needs of everyone.

Old and new forms of church are both called to be mission-shaped and to work together in mission within the rural context. The next section outlines how existing rural churches, old and new, are already responding to the very important developments in rural culture outlined in Chapter 2. It also considers how this ministry might develop and where more fresh expressions of church may be needed to connect with rural people who for some reason do not connect with the ministry of their parish church.

Examples of inculturation – responding to rural cultural distinctives and cultural change

Responding to agriculture

There are some outstanding examples of Christian ministry in the farming community. Perhaps the best known is the Farm Crisis Network, which has been developed since 1993 to help families in farming and related activities who are experiencing problems. It has been described as 'like a Samaritans for farmers', since it has as a prominent part of its ministry a telephone helpline. However, the Farm Crisis Network goes beyond listening on the telephone; local groups of Christians offer a combination of technical and pastoral understanding and individuals from these groups visit farmers in response to need. Some of these are agricultural chaplains, and rural clergy; others are Christian farmers and agricultural specialists. The service reflects its motto, 'Folk who know farming, talking with farming folk'. Through the Arthur Rank Centre, churches of the mainline denominations were also heavily involved in setting up funds to help farmers in crisis due to swine fever, BSE and Foot and Mouth. Quality research on the ethical, environmental, economic and theological issues facing farming is also made accessible through the Arthur Rank Centre and the Agriculture and Theology Project.

These are fantastic mission and ministry projects and yet there would seem to be a gap: In 2006, in the first General Synod debate on the rural church in fifteen years, one farmer commented, 'We aren't yet able to find a way of connecting with the spiritual needs of farmers.'[11] I first started to think about this issue during the Beef Crisis in 1998.

Beef Crisis Sunday

Mrs Ganderton – a remarkable Christian widow farmer – announced, 'Well, all we can do about this Beef Crisis is pray.' We decided to hold 'Beef Crisis Sunday' in her parish church of Broadwas-on-Teme on the Sunday before the first Countryside March in London.[12] She invited everyone she knew to come and pray and we went on the local radio. When 'Beef Crisis Sunday' arrived, the church was packed with Worcestershire and Herefordshire farmers. We sang traditional hymns, we listened to farmers speak of the difficulties and lit candles in prayer.

There was a deep sense of God meeting us in the real struggles of daily life – and a sense of the non-farming villagers growing in understanding for local farmers. However, we didn't follow this up in any way. I still wonder what could have happened if the church had stayed closer in touch with the many farmers who came for prayer and support on that day.

I have come to believe that there is a need for agricultural-mission shaped churches which are distinctive because their identity, worship and *modus operandi* is deeply shaped by their mission in the farming community. In previous centuries, when entire villages worked on the land, many rural parish churches might have been described appropriately in these terms, but in researching this book I have not found any. Often farmers are deeply attached to the history of their own village and church – but farming lifestyle does not make Sunday attendance easy. In addition, those involved in agriculture are increasingly in a minority in rural communities and as we have noted, farmers can often be culturally quite isolated from others in their village. In other words, church life naturally tends to form around the needs of those in a majority.

There are active networks of Christian farmers who engage in mission together and this may suggest that a church based on farming networks would be a fruitful development, enabling the church to reach and support many who currently slip through the parish net. The story of Farm Groups in Devon may point in this direction:

Farm groups

In 2002, Nick Viney was appointed by Exeter Diocese to be 'Farm Groups Project Coordinator'. The idea was to help farmers to support each other, especially in the wake of various agricultural crises from swine fever, BSE to Foot and Mouth. The funding came from Primary Care Trusts, with the goal of reducing suicide rates, which are phenomenally high in the farming community. Nick was supposed to set up support groups – but it became clear early on that such a title and narrow remit would put people off. A broader remit was needed – to have fun, to learn, to broaden outlooks and meet new people as well as share problems and solutions.

Even so, Nick found it difficult to get the groups going until he found three farming couples who prayed together and formed the core of the first group. The key was to pray for the area and to hand over control to God. The group began to thrive and grow as the core invited other farmers. It engaged in a variety of activities – social events, eating together, inviting relevant speakers and farm walks – which offer particular opportunities for unobtrusive pastoral support as well as learning from each other's livelihood options. There are two annual events – a meeting of core leaders to pray and plan and a conference open to all at which the Christian basis of the groups is shared.

Many of these groups are simply friendship and support groups with a praying core . . . but some groups now are exploring a more deliberate examination of faith issues within the group without requiring Christian belief of members. This sounds remarkably like a formula for a farming-based cell church.[13] It will be interesting to see if anything develops in this direction.

Responding to environmental issues

'To strive to safeguard the integrity of creation and sustain and renew the earth'[14] is one of the five marks of mission. Increasing environmental concern is also a feature of our culture and responsiveness to this has potential also to lead to community building activities around which Christian community might form.

A Rocha

A Rocha is a Christian environmental organization, the name coming from the Portuguese for 'the Rock', as the first initiative was a field study centre near the Alvor Estuary in Portugal. As Christians all over the world have recognized the urgent need to protect and restore important habitats, A Rocha has become a family of projects working in Europe, the Middle East, Africa, North and South America and Asia. Most projects have attendant Christian communities based on five values: Christian, Conservation, Community, Cross-cultural and Co-operation. Some A Rocha communities have their own worship, outreach and engagement with the local community and could be thought of as having some similarities to new monastic communities and 'fresh expressions' of church in their own right. A Rocha UK's first community is in an urban situation – but the vision, and the example of A Rocha International includes rural Christian communities caring for the environment and living out a sustainable Christian vision.[15]

Eco-Congregation

Eco-Congregation developed from a partnership between the government-funded environmental charity ENCAMS and the Environmental Issues Network of Churches Together in Britain and Ireland. It aims to encourage churches to consider environmental issues within a Christian context and enable local churches to make positive contributions in their life and mission.

It provides resources and support to green the mission of the local church including: worship; ideas and activities for children and youth; practical advice to care for church premises, grounds and land; information to enable the greening of personal lifestyles; ideas to help churches work with, through and for their local community; resources to help churches act as responsible global neighbours.[16]

Responding to tourism

There are numerous projects across the country aimed at keeping rural church buildings open as places where tourists can stop and find God in the stillness of a sacred space. This is good in itself and at first it might seem that this is all a rural church can do. After all, tourists are passing through. The church building can offer them the opportunity to worship, to find out more; but fleeting contacts offer little opportunity for the nurturing of disciples in community, which is essential to being a mission-shaped church.

On second thoughts, tourism can offer the church the opportunity to serve its local community, working with them to support tourism and economic development in the local area.

Hidden Britain Centres

Hidden Britain Centres[17] are a new community-based tourism project pioneered with the support of the Arthur Rank Centre. The word 'centre' does not refer to a building but to an area where tourists and local community interact.

As part of this initiative, the Bier Room at St Andrew's Church, Dent, has been transformed into the Discover Dentdale visitors' centre open all year round with key church leaders on the management team. Vicar Peter Boyle says,

'There were two main motivations in the PCC's thinking. One was a desire for the parish church to engage with the community, that the parish church should be truly the heart of the community. Secondly, that the church should be good news to the economic life of the community in the aftermath of the recession in the tourist industry following the Foot and Mouth year in 2001. What the Discover Dentdale centre does is provide the tourist industry in Dentdale with infrastructure. It gives the visitor that vital initial welcome and point of contact that encourages them to linger and discover the dale and hopefully, of course, to patronize local businesses along the way.'

When a church involves itself deeply in a community development project like this, the question is whether it can use the opportunity to be reshaped by its new-found mission so that fresh doors open up for new people to discover faith and be nurtured in discipleship. At St Andrew's, Dent, this has begun to happen. The church became keen for the visitor to discover the worship area of the church as a sanctuary and sacred space quite distinctly different from the Centre. A large crucifix has become the central symbol in the church to signal that here is a place of pilgrimage and prayer, not a religious museum, and service times have been altered to be more accessible to visitors. The PCC has been inspired to develop the south aisle area of the church as a special quiet area where people can pray, meditate, light a candle as a act of prayer and piety, and a bookstall encourages people to find out more about the faith. Vicar Peter Boyle is delighted with what is happening:

> I think the centre helps us focus on how to use the church building as a centre for reaching out to people, not only in our community, but to everyone who visits us from around the world; that we have opportunities to proclaim the catholic faith to a great number of pilgrims. It is a privileged position to be in, but it is also an apostolic responsibility.[18]

The phenomena of tourists and rural dwellers alike seeking 'retreat, revival, recreation and risk'[19] in the countryside can prompt fresh missionary initiative. Fresh expressions of church can seek to engage with some of the thousands of people who spend their weekends in rural areas engaging in recreational activities. The story below relates to the seed of a network fresh expression of church, built round an extreme sports community that is active in both rural and urban settings. The distance of this particular subculture from the 'normal' culture of rural church makes this example speak exceptionally clearly about the kind of intense listening which is needed in this kind of mission. Similar principles would apply in the missionary formation of network church around more typically rural activities such as rambling or fishing.

Rezurgence

story story story story

Will New had been considering ordination in the Church of England, but as he began to explore his sense of call, he realized that he would be a square peg in a round hole. His heart was with mountain biking and BMX riding communities where people often see faith as 'a conformist churchy thing' and want little or nothing to do with it. Then, praying with some fellow mountain bikers and BMX riders, 'Rezurgence' was born. The vision was to bring together a passion for riding, faith and living that faith.

Like many contemporary fresh expressions of church, 'Rezurgence' would start with a service – not a church service – but a practical service that would enable bikers to see and be touched by the reality of Jesus. A team was formed, Will employed, and charitable status for the initiative was sought.

In 2005, they set up www.rezurgence.com as a purely rider-run web site that offers high quality positive, reliable information for mountain bike and BMX riders. This was a first for the sport and hits for 2006 are expected to be more than 100,000 a month. The next step is to do something on the field, on the hill or in the skatepark – establishing a presence at events offering a treatment zone for massage/sports therapy and a chill out zone, perhaps even a kit washing and drying service. The ethos of Rezurgence is 'non-conformist, non-forceful and non-evasive'. In other words, they don't conform to the Christian stereotypes: 'No woolly jumpers with leather patches here.'[20] Faith will not be preached at people – the service is unconditional – but they are open about being Christian and ready to respond to those who want to find out more about faith. All this is backed up by regular committed prayer by the ten folk on the Rezurgence team.

Rezurgence does not look very much like a church. Indeed, it wouldn't claim to be one. But it does look very much like the initial fragile missionary engagement in a foreign culture – listening very carefully to the people and to God; seeking to respond with culturally appropriate service. Will is quick to recognize that if bikers want to explore faith, they are likely to be reluctant to be redirected to their local parish church – the establishing of a Christian basics course, worship or cells may not be so very far away.

While some seek recreation in the countryside, others seek sacred space, stillness, reconnecting with nature and a simple yet deep spirituality. This is the sort of contemporary longing that the network church 'Contemplative Fire', launched in 2004, seeks to address.

Contemplative Fire

Contemplative Fire describes itself as 'a journey into the present moment, an exploration of a great spiritual tradition as it impacts life in the twenty-first century.' In October 2005, their website reads:

'How can we have access to the spiritual treasure that lies at the heart of the teachings on the way of Christ? By experiencing their inscape, their interior dynamic and by allowing this energy to transfigure our life, our work and relationships. Contemplative Fire seeks to provide opportunities at many levels for personal and group work to enable us to enter deeply into the understanding of Jesus and the Christian mystics.

In local and regional gatherings for stillness and storytelling, for the playful as well as the profound, Contemplative Fire seeks to avoid the allure of easy answers and the lust for certitude. We celebrate the sacrament of the present moment in the beauty of nature, in contemplative liturgy and teaching.'[21]

Contemplative Fire is not an exclusively rural expression of church. It is a network of people, rural and urban, seeking a particular kind of spirituality. However, it is notable that many of its events are held in rural settings. Founder Philip Roderick feels that this reflects the practice of Jesus who often withdrew to beautiful remote areas in order to pray. Every other month, a four-hour 'pilgrimage to now/here' with teachings from the Christian mystics takes place on a beautiful 400 acre estate with participants taking a 'walk of awareness' through fields and woods. 'The Gathering', a monthly reflective Eucharist, began in a tiny remote rural church and when it outgrew this venue moved to a converted barn. This is not so much tapping into current tourist visits to the countryside as responding to some of the buried longings which attract people to the countryside.

Responding to population shift

The realization that so many rural dwellers originated in the towns can help us to recognize that some of the forms of church which we may have previously dismissed as urban or suburban phenomena, may actually now be equally as culturally appropriate in the countryside. In Chapter 5, we will see that every category of 'fresh expression' explored by the *Mission-shaped Church* report[22] is capable of a rural version. The constraints on the building of different kinds of fresh expressions seem to come more from the constraints on resources in the rural setting and from the nature of Anglican church structures, than from the nature of the rural context. This is exemplified by the Fountain of Life, which is able to respond to quite different missionary opportunities than the multi-parish benefices among which it is set.

The Fountain of Life

The Fountain of Life is a Missionary Congregation of the Church of England situated in rural mid-Norfolk. It has no parish. Its mission is to the networks of friends of existing members with some specific missionary initiatives designed to reach out to specific cultural networks that have little relationship with local parish churches. The congregation is a mixture of new converts who have little church background and those who have been raised in various church traditions but feel that the new church is where they belong. There is a balance between 'incomers' to the rural scene and 'old villagers', with a few people from non-rural areas.

As a church the Fountain of Life has the qualities and facilities normally associated with popular town churches – prayerfulness, inspiring worship with good music, high quality children's and youth work, a programme for enquirers, a full time minister dedicated to this congregation alone, loving relationships, pastoral care, a warm comfortable venue, adequate finance from the giving of the congregation. The church is growing by word of mouth and is clearly the sort of community to which members feel able to invite rural-dwelling non-Christian friends.

In some rural areas, a congregation like Fountain of Life might not be an appropriate response to population shift. Where population shift is recent or conflict between new and old villagers is marked, reconciliation may need to be given a high priority in mission and make a network approach inappropriate. However, evidence suggests that in many areas of the countryside, reconciliation to a major social change has already taken place with incomers being in a majority.[23] It is important that in our shaping of church we recognize the new reality of the mission context as it is.

Responding to reduced social capital

The churches collectively are the largest and oldest voluntary organization in the countryside and are already a focal point in many local communities for the building of social capital – 'encouraging local people to lead on reducing their isolation and boosting their own economies'.[24] There is a marked difference in the way the rural church and the urban church tend to serve their communities. Urban churches are more likely to have large church-based projects whereas in rural areas we see individual Christians involved in community projects such as meals-on-wheels, Age Concern, local parent-and-toddler groups.[25] One of the advantages of this is that 'there is a huge overlap between church and community in rural areas in a way not often found in urban areas'.[26]

The downside is that Christian service is often rendered invisible. Christians thinly spread in very small churches may not undertake church-run initiatives more because they feel they have not got the capacity rather than because there is no felt need. The story of Hollybush Christian Fellowship, planted in 1968, illustrates what is possible when rural Christians over a wide area come together:

Hollybush Christian Fellowship

Hollybush Christian Fellowship is situated in the farmyard of Jim Wilkinson in the remote hamlet of Newsham near Thirsk in Yorkshire. It started from a vision that the farm would be 'an oasis in the desert, a place where people would come from the North, South, East and West to minister and to be ministered to. A place of refreshing, healing and deliverance.' Hollybush deliberately seeks to meet people who are not part of a church congregation in their physical, mental, emotional and spiritual needs.

Starting from small beginnings, today the congregation of over 200 is composed of people from all denominations and none. There is a core team of six, three of whom are paid. The fellowship receives referrals from social services and local doctors' surgeries – some for practical help and some for pastoral care. There is a used clothing store open 2–3 days a week. There is a programme for children – including holiday projects and seasonal workshops. Hollybush hosts four summer youth camps for young people from Lancashire schools and several more open to all. The annual camp for families attracts 800 people. There is a café on site which caters for parties, anniversaries and special events. The café is open all day during the summer camps. Volunteers from Hollybush are also active in visiting a local prison, hospital visiting and the Church Army youth bus project in Thirsk. The church responds to need. During the Foot and Mouth crisis, it sent a letter of support and prayer to every farm within six miles of the centre, to the appreciation of many.[27]

Undoubtedly, there is room for many more larger churches working in this way in the countryside. However, small church initiatives can be much more powerful than is often recognized. Initiatives such as a lift scheme, a senior citizens' lunch club, a bereavement group, an after school club, a farmers' market may be within the reach of quite small Christian communities working in partnership with others and the very smallness and vulnerability of rural Christian communities may help in the building of social capital.[28]

Stronger, larger churches may be able to have professionally run programmes, but there is a danger that they become a project for enthusiasts – rather than integral to the life of the Christian community. More needs may be met, but the very focus on needs meeting can lead to the loss of the potentially transforming process of engaging in a struggle alongside those in need. 'Needs meeting' puts the church in a position of superiority; participation in a struggle puts the church alongside people. As Ann Morisey has pointed out, 'when both we and the other are empty handed, then we become party to a cascade of grace'.[29] Struggling together, the helped and the helpers discover their brotherhood – and both find their lives transformed by the gospel.

The challenge for a smaller church, involved in projects which build social capital, is whether these projects are kept in a separate compartment – not affecting the worship, teaching and fellowship of the church – or whether the church community will choose to be more deeply transformed by its new-found mission, so that it is shaped for new people to discover faith and be nurtured in discipleship.

Finally, responding to the need for the rebuilding of social capital may not be through specific projects at all. At heart, the need is for the church community to practise the building of deep relationships – within its own community, with the stranger and even with those whom we perceive as a threat in some way.[30] Relationships are at the heart of the emerging church movement but this emphasis deserves to belong to all expressions of church – old and new. As Dr Peter Carruthers of the Countryside Agency commented in 2003:

> If I had to highlight one feature of the rural landscape, and one challenge to the Church it would be the issue of relationships. At the heart of rural society, and indeed at the heart of society in general, is a huge relational deficit . . . Yet we Christians should be 'experts' in relationships. We are called to love God and love neighbour – on which hang everything else (Matthew 22.34-40). Relationships are the unifying idea! And our understanding of mission reflects this – evangelism, social responsibility, care of creation.[31]

Responding to national trends in the rural context – coming to terms with the reality of network

Some rural ministers feel that the focus on network in the *Mission-shaped Church* report makes it less relevant in the countryside. They tell me that in rural areas the traditional local church model ought to be recognized as prior. This is partly correct in the sense that, at the present time, parish/locality-based expressions of church retain more cultural relevance in rural than in urban areas. However, the great strength of the *Mission-shaped Church* report is that it recognizes neither network nor parish as prior. What is prior is participating in God's mission in the culture to which we have been sent, whatever that may be, local or network or (usually) a combination of the two.[32] 'At its best the parochial system is founded upon a vision of Christian community in the service of a wider society that is in itself a means of mission.'[33] It is the same principle of serious engagement with the surrounding society that is intended by the parish system, which inspires truly mission-shaped fresh expressions of church whether based on locality or network.

A more weighty critique of the formation of such network-based churches is whether this constitutes embracing a cultural reality, which ought rather to be resisted. The network society has many casualties. As community is increasingly formed around networks rather than locality, those people who are unable to be mobile will find themselves in no community at all due to the weakening of the neighbourhood as a friendship base. These people are often the most vulnerable in our society; elderly people, those without jobs or cars, those suffering from long-term illness.

In this situation, the vision of the parish church congregation embracing all ages and groups within the community and caring for all within the parish bounds is impressively countercultural. However, it is difficult to find actual parish churches that truly represent the social composition of their locality. More often than not it is those aged 10–40, especially men and boys and the less well off, who are underrepresented. When the young and less affluent are in a minority, their voices are often not heard. 'We go to all the services the choir sings in,' complained a small group of teenagers at a church away day, 'but when it comes to the family service, they don't support us.' Nothing changed. Two years later, only one of that group still attends church.

Nine years ago as a rural curate, I reacted angrily to a seminar at which Graham Cray talked about the homogenous unit principle[34] in relation to youth mission: 'He should try working in the countryside,' I cried, 'How in a village of 300 souls can anyone hope to form a youth congregation? In any case, what about the gospel breaking down barriers between people? What about the body of Christ?' By the end of my curacy, I had to admit it was only 'JAM' – the cluster of youth cells in the rural half of the deanery – which had enabled many young people to come to faith and stay in touch with the scattered adult congregations. There is more than one way of being a heterogenous body of Christ. It doesn't have to involve everyone meeting together every Sunday morning and worshipping in the same style. In fact this might be the least helpful way in which to demonstrate our unity, resulting in culture wars or the pressure of constant compromise. If church is not only about the dimension of worship but also community and mission, the unity of the body may be more easily expressed in shared meals or shared social action. In the case of 'JAM', the youth invited local church members to meals at which their youth band performed. This led to invitations to the band to contribute to worship in family services round the deanery – and so the youth were able to both gain strength from meeting with other young people and offer a distinctive ministry within a wider church family. Offering people the freedom to explore issues of faith, and experience a significant part of church life in company with people with whom they share much in common, can eventually lead to an overall more diverse and mutually accepting church family.

A further reason for the tendency to baulk at the reality of networks in the countryside is that a deep-rootedness and sense of place has been long considered one of the special gifts which rural life and church offers to a predominantly urban society.[35] Brueggemann, for example, has written of the failed 'urban promise' concerning 'human persons who could lead detatched, unrooted lives of endless choice and no commitment . . . glamourized around the virtues of mobility and anonymity which seem so full of freedom and self-actualisation'.[36] By contrast, rural attachment to the land has brought stability and a sense of responsibility to neighbours, to forebears and to those who will follow.

It is, of course, right that the Church should mourn at the arrival of a shallower more consumerist culture which is invading the countryside through urban-rural drift and the urban-orientated media, but we should not refuse to speak God's word within the networks where this culture thrives. Indeed, most rural church members already live lives pervaded by the network reality. Such networks, often centred outside the parish on the school gate, social and cultural activities, the office, the pub, the supermarket or the livestock market, are seen by rural dwellers as normal and natural, not as disloyal to the village of residence. The average multi-parish benefice is already well equipped with traditional village churches. Alongside these, within the 'mixed economy', there is a need to develop more expressions of church that are shaped by the network aspects of rural life. As Archbishop Rowan Williams has written:

> So far from living in the afterglow of a golden age of rural piety that has characterized the greater part of Christian history, it would be more accurate to say that rural faith is still finding its distinctive voice. And that cannot be resolved, by importing styles and structures formed in other settings. The current economic and social challenges are enormous . . . but happily . . . the response of the churches is increasingly serious and creative, conscious of the diversity of rural lives. We can reasonably hope that ahead of us lies a new level of engagement with mission in this environment.[37]

Responding to the interweaving of many factors in rural culture

In this chapter, church stories have been grouped under headings representing aspects of the mission context to which they respond. This reflects something of the proper order of things; showing how church must be shaped by mission and the context of that mission. However, it is over-simplistic: churches must respond to more than one aspect of the mission context at once. The next chapter looks at common types of 'fresh expression' to see how these potentially respond to a complex interweaving of various cultural factors. This enables some comparison to be made with similar forms of church in urban or suburban contexts to see what is distinctively rural.

4 Rural fresh expressions

This chapter falls into two parts. The first looks at the variety of 'fresh expression' identified by the *Mission-shaped Church* report, giving rural examples for each. In this part, the following categories are explored:

- alternative worship communities
- base ecclesial communities
- café church
- cell church
- churches arising out of community initiatives
- midweek congregations
- multiple congregations
- network-focused churches
- school-based churches
- seeker church
- traditional church plants
- youth congregations.

The working group never intended this to be an exhaustive list so much as an indication of key themes and ideas. However, by using this list as a starting-point, it is easier to reflect on the differences that arise in the form these fresh expressions take in the rural context compared to urban and suburban expressions.

The second, shorter, part of the chapter is concerned with 'traditional forms of church inspiring new interest',[1] which is of particular relevance in rural contexts.

A variety of fresh expressions

Alternative worship communities

'Alt. worship' groups attempt to relate worship and certain strands of post-modern culture. They are characterized by the *Mission-shaped Church* report as 'being in touch with preferences for ambiguity and antiquity'.[2] Alternative worship events often use a multimedia approach. Nationally, these groups tend to be dominated by those who are dissatisfied in some way with existing church and so may act as a sort of safety net – but they do not seem to attract many people who were previously nonchurched.

> ### The Gathering
>
> story
> story
> story
> story
>
> 'The Gathering'[3] at a remote barn in the Buckinghamshire village of Wiggington could be described as a kind of alternative worship.[4] Music from Russian Orthodox to Afro-Celtic is provided by a good sound system. There is no sermon, no written liturgy. The shape of the service is provided by simple chant, silence and symbols. This does not mean there are no words. Words come from Scripture, from the writings of mystics and poets and from spoken reflection. There is an interweaving of complex themes rather than a single focus. The language is intelligent and sophisticated; suited to a mainly educated and relatively affluent congregation, but non-didactic and open-ended. The symbols are considerably less hi-tech than the visuals normally associated with alt. worship and many draw deeply on the natural, rural setting – wood, stone and earth, wind and sky; the beams of the old barn, grain, flowers, candlelight. Learning to contemplate the presence of God in and through particular tangible things, we begin to recognize his presence everywhere.
>
> Like alternative worship in urban settings, 'The Gathering' currently has a congregation in which the greater number of people have previous significant experience of church. The

vision, however, is to reach out to nonchurched people who wish to explore spirituality but who might experience the established Church as lacking in depth, and this is beginning to happen. Unlike some other alt. worship groups, 'The Gathering' is only one element of the fresh expression of church that is Contemplative Fire. Through a bi-monthly 'pilgrimage to now/here' and various training events, there is a real enabling of participants to live the Christian faith at a deeper level. The community of *peregrini* (pilgrims) commit themselves to a rhythm of life, and contemplation-in-action.

'The Gathering' illustrates that not all people living in rural areas prefer 'traditional' worship. In fact, many rural parish churches have experimented successfully with occasional alt. worship events.

One important key to consider is the nature of the spirituality of the people we wish to be involved. The sophisticated language of Contemplative Fire is well suited to the area around London populated by many well-educated professionals. However, in other parts of the country, it is often part of indigenous rural culture of folk to place a particularly high value on the virtues of being down to earth and unpretentious. In such areas, 'The Gathering' might be perceived as wordy or contrived. Here, contextualized alt. worship would probably draw less strongly on material from different cultures, while retaining and developing the emphasis on the local – the local natural environment, local churches and holy sites, local art and music.

Similarly, many rural areas will lack financial resources and people to operate sophisticated technological equipment. However, there are resources suited to alt. worship, particularly or uniquely available in rural areas:

- evocative venues such as small remote churches where candles are the only available form of light, church ruins, a windmill, an ancient well;
- silence and the sounds of nature;
- the night sky, without light pollution;

- projected pictures of local natural scenes;

- stories and writings of local saints;

- produce from local farms and gardens;

- the experiences of people who, through tending livestock, live closely with the cycles of life and death and have much to contribute to a death-denying culture;

- contributions from a local artist or craftsman;

- the more obvious passage of the seasons in the landscape.

Postmodern culture is deeply attracted by the mystical. To many parts of society, mystery must not be too directly explained and symbols speak more eloquently than many words. Some contemporary worship services seem out of touch with the postmodern desire for spiritual experience beyond words. There is enormous potential to develop simple forms of worship in the countryside that reflect a deep wonder at God's creation.

Base ecclesial communities

Base ecclesial communities (BECs) originated in Roman Catholic Latin America as a way of being church. They were a particular response to the shortage of priests and the large numbers of poor. They are small groups whose biblical, prayerful reflection leading to action is central to their common life as church. Life is not compartmentalized into 'sacred' and secular', rather, biblical reflection begins with the reality of life as experienced and leads the community to act together to bring about the reign of God in the world. A BEC in Latin America might set up a small workshop to refurbish worn out shoes, run a home for the homeless elderly or seek together fairer working conditions. A BEC is a church of the poor, for the poor. In this country, BECs have mainly been associated with Urban Priority Areas. The *Mission-shaped Church* report told the story of how BECs were introduced in the parishes of St Michael and St Barnabas, Plymouth with a number of community projects resulting including a programme to enable disadvantaged young people to learn to sail. In June 2000, John Summers, one of the clergy who had led these churches, retired to the South Hams of Devon. This is his description of what happened in the small village of Rattery (pop. 500) about 4 miles from where he lived.

Rattery BEC

Sunday attendance depended upon which liturgy was on offer. At 1662 Communion or Matins there might be 12 or 15 present. For a more modern service there might be between 6 and 10 on a good day. With a varied menu on Sunday evenings, support varied between 2 and 6. A monthly family service had been started by the vicar, but was now usually led by the two very active and imaginative Readers, when perhaps up to 30 or so joined in. Overall the parish had a very traditional feel. The groups of worshippers seemed disconnected from one another. I was asked to help with the communion services and I discovered the people to be warm, hospitable and, crucially, open to new ways of thinking and doing things. They realized that without change the church would continue to shrink and die. So in 2001 I was asked to introduce the ideas of a 'New Way of Being Church' as a four-week Advent course.

We were welcomed into the home of a retired farmer and his wife where a group had been meeting for a Bible study. We gathered in their large Rayburn-heated kitchen for a cuppa. We began by lighting a candle to remind us that 'the Lord is here' and that His Spirit is with us'. We then, in turn, share personal, local and world news. The next step is to decide upon a passage of the Bible, which seems to relate to the issues raised in the 'news'. More often, we use the lectionary reading for the following Sunday. This is then used as a basis for prayerful reflection, so that we might discern what God might be saying to us and wanting us to do, to make a difference in our own context.[5]

BECs usually use a 5- or 7-step process[6] to engage with the Bible that enables everyone to make a contribution, and prevents any one person imposing their own agenda on the group. It is flexible and simple; following the pastoral cycle of see–reflect–act. The group shares responsibility for its proper functioning through tasks such as hospitality, memory, time-keeping, prayer and worship and, vitally, the role of co-ordination of the group to enable them to function together without being dependent upon a 'leader'. John Summers' reflections show that BECs are far more than a Bible study group and constitute a new way of being church:

> The key is that we are coming together as 'church' (not just as individuals) to read and prayerfully reflect upon the Bible in the presence of the Holy Spirit, in the context of our every day experience, to try to discern what the Spirit is saying to the church. We are developing a wider awareness of our local community and are learning new ways to be agents of change towards the kingdom of God. For example, just before the Queen's Jubilee, it became known that a special celebration event in the village had been cancelled, so the two church-wardens raised the issue at the Tuesday group and got folk together to organize a fun day for the whole village.[7]

Café church

Church services with high quality music and a well-presented ministry of the word have been compared to theatre. In contrast, 'café church' describes churches which seek to develop the ambience of a café – gathering around tables, rather than sitting in an 'audience' – creating a greater sense of community. Food is an essential part of the experience rather than an add-on at the end of a service.

Café Church in Thorndon

Thorndon is a village of fewer than 650 people in East Anglia with a typical small rural church occupied by a typically small rural congregation. Church members wanted to have a gathering which would encourage people who never came to church to feel welcome, unthreatened and relaxed. After much prayer and discussion, based on heartfelt concern for the village community, café church was born. Rector David Clayden writes:

We deliberately steered away from the term 'service'. People gather in the church at about 10am on the third Sunday of the month. The building is warm, they are greeted by the aroma of real coffee and hot croissants, and a whole lot of meeting and greeting takes place. Around 10.30 folks move to the pews and an interactive Christian drama takes place involving adults and children of all ages (now known as the Parable Players). Much is ad lib with narrators telling the Bible story while others act it out – there is always much fun and laughter.

This is followed by a simple explanation of the meaning and relevance of the drama. Prayers take place involving adults and children, followed by a worship song and dismissal. All this is led by elders, churchwardens and lay folk. The rector, having a nine parish multi-parish benefice, only gets to café church if a baptism is requested. Café church has been in existence for 16 months with attendances around 49 including children.[8]

At Thorndon, café church includes worship, but in café churches this would be a greater element as in this story of a breakfast café event in Milverton, a medium-size village of around 1,500 people lying in the very outskirts of Taunton in Somerset.

Sunday Starts Here

Each year, for about a fortnight around the May Bank holiday weekend, the various societies in the village of Milverton put on arts and social events that attract many of the locals and some beyond. Back in 2000, as part of the parish church's contribution to this, the congregation hosted traditional full English Breakfasts in the church hall prior to holding a service celebrating the life of the village in the church. The response to the breakfasts was overwhelming and this led the PCC to think. They perceived that many saw Sunday as a day of relaxation, to be with their family and/or a day into which they eased themselves with the Sunday newspaper. The 'Sunday Starts Here' project responds to this reality about Sundays.

SSH (as it has come to be known) is a monthly event. From 9.15 a.m. onwards continental-style breakfasts are served and are attended both by those who stay on from an early service and those who are coming to SSH itself. The Sunday newspapers are provided and activities in the forms of treasure hunts, craft making and quizzes, often relating to the theme of the service to come and making use of the whole church space, are available for the children to enjoy once they've eaten their breakfast. At 10.00 a.m. there is a short service (lasting an absolute maximum of 40 minutes) which utilizes a music group specially formed for the project and lively and more modern music. The service is largely non-liturgical and makes use of video, drama and non-biblical material as well readings from Scripture and interactive forms of prayer such lighting candles, making prayer balloons or prayer cairns. Themes have varied from asking some of the big questions about life and God (How do we know he exists?) to a series run on the Ten Commandments which different families took it in turns to lead.

SSH attracts, on average, around 50 people who are mainly families with children from the local primary school who do not attend church at any other time, together with a few regular churchgoers. Other members of the usual congregation are linked with it through the shared breakfast and regard it as an essential part of their outreach. However, it also feels separate from what constitutes church life the rest of the time.

In my research, it has been easier to find various shades of café church in the countryside than any other kind of fresh expression. Perhaps café church is a particularly attractive concept in rural areas, where there may be a shortage of places to meet socially over a coffee. Another example in this book is that of *Cafeplus+*, described in Chapters 5 and 6. All of these have something of the nature of an outsider's taste and see gathering about them. They respond to the social reality of Sunday as a day for family and relaxation. The challenge is how to enable those who enthusiastically attend these monthly events to move into deeper discipleship.

Cell church

Cells are vital units of the body – and cells in church life are small groups (6–14 members in each), which contain the DNA of what it means to be church. The model originated in South East Asia – as a way of coping with the growth of the church – but is now well established in many cultures across the world. A cell church is a 'church without walls', seeing its primary identity in these small groups although both the 'big wing' and the 'small wing' are seen as necessary. The 'big wing' is often (but not always) expressed in Sunday congregational worship. Cells are based on a few key values,[9] which are phrased differently in different churches but broadly tend to include:

- Jesus at the centre – meeting with Jesus at the core;

- every member in ministry – everyone with a role to play;

- personal growth – everyone taking responsibility for their personal holiness and growth in Christ;

- multiplication – by spreading the gospel and making disciples, one cell grows and becomes two cells. Everyone is involved in making God known;

- community – building strong relationships, inside and outside cell;

- sacrificial love – unconditional love, modelled on the love of Jesus;

- honesty – the doorway to community, accountability and Christian growth.

The radical application of these values and the emphasis that a cell is church in miniature is what makes cell church very different from a church with home groups.

An increasing number of Anglican rural churches and multi-parish benefices practise cells that may be based on network[10] or on geographical areas. It may be that cells work particularly well in the rural context because small numbers are already seen as normal and good both for church and other community activities. In an Anglican context, cells can work as a parallel structure alongside parish church as in the case of the Tas Valley Cell Church whose story is told in the Prologue.[11] Below, we look at an example of a non-denominational cell church. This enables us to look at the different potential of cell church if separated more completely from parish structures.

story
story
story
story

Threshold

Threshold started as a single cell in 1995 in rural Lincolnshire. They collaborate closely with other denominations and seek to be a community where people not used to church will feel at home and can explore Christianity in an open, non-threatening way. In addition to the standard cell church values Threshold stands for accessibility, generosity and hospitality. Witness in each village begins with neighbourliness, barbeques, parties and practical help.

Over ten years, it has grown to over two hundred members. The cells are now grouped into 'clusters' that provide a local focus, to see the values of God's kingdom increasingly established and expressed in the life of particular neighbour-hoods. There are three 'clusters' in the village of Nettleham, one in Welton/Dunholme, one in Wragby and one in the Monks Road area of Lincoln. Each has their own style – some have more emphasis on families, others on community service. There is a youth wing with cells and youth worship and a creative arts group. Most clusters meet together on alternate Sundays and on the intervening Sundays the whole church gathers for a celebration, currently at William Farr School, Welton.

The cell structure, developed separately from parish congregations, enables even more flexibility within a uniting framework of shared values. Local initiatives can develop in ways that are appropriate to their setting without imposing a one-size-fits-all model for ministry. The cells themselves provide a supportive environment in which to come closer to God through study, prayer and worship. They also enable leadership development. Around half of Threshold's adult members are involved in leading a cell or group with responsibility for worship, children's ministry or mission.

Churches arising out of community initiatives

Typically, churches begun as a result of community initiatives have been in urban areas of deprivation among people who are far from the culture of traditional church. In most instances these initiatives have not started with a deliberate attempt to create church, but as trust has built up there has been a curiosity about the values of Christians that led to the initiative. As people have grown into disciples, it has become apparent that a new church has to be shaped to be appropriate to the culture of the new disciples.

The rural situation is often very different from this, for the church is very frequently already important in the community. The church building may even be the last community building in the village. In the countryside, we might expect community initiatives often to start with use of the church building. This would lead us to expect not so much a new church but, as in the two examples given below, an opportunity for the existing church community to be renewed and reshaped within its new facilities by its new-found mission.[12]

---

story
story
story
story

Post Church

On Maundy Thursday 2004, people in Sheepy Magna pondered the servanthood of Jesus washing his disciples' feet and opened a new satellite post office in the base of the church tower. The project involved major changes to the church building including the provision of water and toilet facilities. The Post Office is open two mornings a week and at the same time refreshments are

served in the new community area. The church sells local
newspapers, bread and confectionary products made by a
local bakery and are about to have a CONNECT computer
point set up so that residents can access information about
county council services on-line. As the facilities at the church
have improved, concerts, singing, a 'mums and toddlers' group,
an art group and other activities have sprung up.[13]

Shipbourne farmers' market

The weekly farmers' market held in St Giles'
Church, Shipbourne, Kent, came about as a result
of a discussion at the PCC on ways in which the church could
respond to the government's Rural White Paper in 2000. The
village shop had closed in 1981 but the gap was still felt. There
was also a realization that the farming community needed
support. Numbers of customers vary from week to week but
average at 150. It is a friendly market with top quality produce
and has become an ideal meeting place for parishioners. The
market is unusual – and may be unique – in that it is run by a
sub-committee of the PCC. The hosting of the market is an
act of service from which the church makes no money: all
profits are divided between farming charities in the UK and
the developing world.[14]

Midweek congregations

The midweek communion service has a long history in both urban and rural
parishes. However, more recently it has been recognized as having a new
significance. Instead of attracting mainly the most committed members of
the Sunday congregation, such services are increasingly attended by those
who cannot or who will not attend on a Sunday. For them, this is their
ecclesial community.

Orwell midweek Eucharists

The benefice of Orwell consists of five rural parishes (Arrington, Barrington, Croydon with Cloton, Orwell and Wimpole) with a combined population of approximately 2,500 adults. The rector, the Revd Neil Brice, has conducted midweek Eucharists outside the church building for the last 14 years. There is one each week, spread among the parishes so that each parish has a midweek Eucharist once a month. After a shortened Eucharist, there is a chance to chat over coffee. There are hymns but no sermon. The 'Ministry of the Word' is often discussion based. The Eucharists take place in various venues including community rooms and homes. Until recently, one monthly Eucharist took place in the public house in Barrington and this attracted an average of 25 people each month. The Revd Neil Brice says:

> 'We have found that those attending these services may be people who cannot get to the church services on a Sunday, maybe because they are elderly or disabled. Some are simply more comfortable in non-church venues. The congregations are mostly ladies who are not at work at the time of the services. We do find that at holiday time (including Bank Holidays) the congregation changes and people normally at work may also join us. These midweek services have broken down a barrier for some who did not use to attend 'normal' Sunday and are now able to do so. There is no doubt in my mind that there has been a sense of fellowship within these services and discipleship is enabled. We are currently planning to start another 'pub' Eucharist or service in the village of Orwell, now that we have ceased using the pub at Barrington. Rather interestingly the congregation have very much missed meeting there!'[15]

Multiple congregations

In large urban churches, different congregations may be deliberately started within the same building to offer different liturgical styles and serve different sociological groups. In rural areas, the multi-parish benefice normally offers multiple services in order to serve different geographical communities. While this is not exactly a new mission strategy, it is vitally important to rural mission and may go part way to explaining why church attendance is proportionately higher in rural areas than in urban ones.

A more unusual pattern of multiple congregations can be found in the Cherwell Valley Benefice in the Diocese of Oxford.

Upper Hayford

Church Army officer Ian Biscoe and his wife Erika came to the old airbase at Upper Hayford in September 2002 to develop church in what was expected to be a new housing development. The development was stalled but 800 people soon took up residence in the old base houses. Rents are cheap and the feel is a bit like a local authority estate. Four age-based congregations have developed based in the old airbase chapel. The first, for adults, began through an Alpha course and has continued to meet on Thursday evenings. 'Kidz Club' meeting on Sunday afternoons features plenty of fun and interaction for younger children. The third and fourth congregations are 'Hey U!' for 11–14s and 'Revival' for older youth. A typical meeting for each 'congregation' involves some time together for age-appropriate input and worship and then divides into smaller cells to go deeper. Three times a year everyone joins together to host a big celebratory event such as a Christmas meal for the wider community. From a population of 800, the multiple congregation approach has enabled over 120 people to be regularly involved in the church. Recently, this fresh expression of church has joined six small parishes in the Cherwell Valley Benefice, adding a new layer to church life.[16]

Network-focused churches

In the countryside, as elsewhere, people are no longer shaping their lives within parochial boundaries. They also inhabit networks, often formed around work, education, leisure interests or artistic preferences. Many parish churches unconsciously serve particular networks because members bring friends and the church becomes shaped by those who feel at home in the style offered in that particular church. Network-focused churches more consciously encourage a 'go and inhabit' approach to particular networks in order that 'gospel and church become a reality among the variety of ways that people are living'.[17] We have seen many examples of this approach in the fresh expressions already described.

Typically network churches deliberately reach into networks where the ministry of the parish church is not present or peripheral, so that they complement parish churches in fulfilling our national calling to be a church for all people. Rezurgence,[18] for example, engages with mountain bikers and BMX riders over a wide area. Contemplative Fire[19] engages with people whose spiritual quest is formed in a particular way. Other kinds of network churches might grow if we sought to engage in inculturation in the agricultural community or Sunday afternoon ramblers.

Network-focused churches do have a 'place' element to them because people's networks are partly defined by the places to which they travel. A youth network church, for example, may be focused on a particular school. In the Tas Valley Benefice, described in the Prologue, some networks – e.g. 'parent and toddler' – do not reach far beyond the benefice. A purely network church would define itself by the focus of the network rather than by a geographical boundary. Many fresh expressions of church like the Tas Valley cell church[20] have a network focus but with some geographical elements and share common characteristics of network churches such as:

- identifying social gatherings and meeting points in order to develop relationships with people in a chosen cultural network;

- small groups where people can experience community, meaning and significance;

- mission expressed through relational evangelism and practical acts of service;

● personal mentoring and personal accountability.[21]

School-based churches

A large proportion of rural primary schools already have a Church of
England Foundation. This means that collective worship (and sometimes RE)
is governed by the Christian trust deed and that the local church is already
represented on the board of governors. It would be unusual for the local
priest or other church members not to be involved in other ways too –
taking assemblies, helping out listening to children read or running after-
school clubs. School-based churches may meet at weekends or after school.
Often they grow out of after-school clubs. The village school is often at the
centre of the community and it is much easier for parents and grandparents
of children at the school to cross the threshold and feel comfortable.
In addition, the geography and superior heating of the building may offer
options for a far wider range of church activities than could be
accommodated in the church building. All this makes school-based churches
a particularly suitable approach in the countryside.

story
story
story
story

The Church in the School

The Church in the School is a rural fresh
expression of church that aims to make the most
of the connection with the church school. Starting from an
existing Sunday school, 'The church in the school' aims to
reach out to parents as well as children at St Stephen's school,
Banks, in Lancashire. It meets most weeks except for a
monthly parade service with the parish church. Worship is
contemporary and child friendly with three groups for infants,
juniors and 11+ and a seeker-focused adult talk. There is also
a midweek small group for discipleship and regular socials
shared with the school and parish church.

Service in the School

Service in the School is exactly what it says on the tin. Since 2003, a group of people from the three Anglican parishes of Whitmore, Maer and Chapel Chorlton in Staffordshire have been planning and leading Sunday services three times a term in Baldwin's Gate school. About 50 adults and 25 children come to the services, most of whom are local families who would not otherwise go to church. Alongside these services there is a weekly children's club in the school. It provides Christian-based activities – art and craft for younger children; music and dance for older children. Over a third of the children in the school attend this club. The long-term hope is to develop a fully-fledged congregation centred on regular worship in the school.

Seeker services

Seeker services do not set out to be a new type of church. They are part of a church programme providing a different way in to church, connecting those who are interested and on the fringes of church with worship and with God. They may provide a bridge either to traditional church or to a fresh expression of church. The seeker approach was founded by Willow Creek Church in Chicago. In its purest form it is very 'resource heavy', using film clips, drama, contemporary music and lots of technical equipment. However, the basic principle of making church services accessible and meaningful to people with little background in Christian worship has been adapted by many rural churches, using simply the resources they have.

First Sunday

In Ditchingham, the church building is a mile outside the village. The PCC decided to move one service a month to neutral ground at the local school and make the style of worship as accessible as possible. They called it 'First Sunday' and drew from the Willow Creek 'seeker service' model. The hall is decorated with brightly coloured banners. People sit round tables and have refreshments and then the service begins, including drama, modern worship and short seeker-friendly talks. First Sunday Youth runs at the same time, allowing the adult service to address relevant themes. At the beginning, personnel for this ministry were drawn from around the benefice but is now more locally based. In the last six years attendance has grown from 20 to 60. The venture has been so appreciated that the idea is spreading round the benefice: the small congregation in Alburgh with 6-12 people, has started a similar service in the new school hall there.[22]

Traditional church plants

Traditional church plants are usually begun within the parish of the sending church as a response to an area not being reached by the ministry of the sending congregation. They are rare in rural areas where parish populations are typically low and the number of congregations per head of population is higher than in urban and suburban areas.[23] However, they may have increasing relevance in areas of new housing. The example below relates to the parish of Anston, which lies in urban shadow east of Sheffield and whose total population is approaching 10,000. The parish church lies in South Anston which is separated from North Anston by a major road. The area of North Anston is predominantly post-war council housing stock while South Anston contains more expensive private housing. These differences meant there was a need for a greater Christian presence in the area of North Anston, centred on the Woodland Drive estate.

Stepping Stones

Stepping Stones[24] began in 1995 with a small planting team from St James's, Anston, under the leadership of the then curate, Steve Millwood. They worked hard to develop all age worship which was relevant to the culture of the people of the area – most of whom were totally unchurched. Over the last eleven years, the church plant has experienced many of the challenges common to traditional church plants – especially that of continuing leadership when the initial pioneer moves on.

Today, the congregation has moved from the church room to the community centre at Woodland Drive and is led by parish evangelists, Sheelagh and Paul Easby. On a typical Sunday thirty adults and a dozen children gather for worship. During the week, there is extensive visiting on the estate and a thriving Kidz Klub. 'Kobblestones' is a weekly afternoon group for those who are 'Knocking-On-a-Bit', where the ladies enjoy friendship, refreshments and Bible study. A fellowship group meets in homes weekly, and a men's group has just begun to meet.

Some new local people are making commitments to Christ and many are growing stronger in faith and discipleship. 'Stepping Stones' remains a daughter church of St James but is also a worshipping and prayerful community in its own right.

Youth congregations

Youth congregations are a kind of network church – led by youth for youth. Their network is the network of schools, youth services and the various youth cultures that may prevail in an area. Despite their homogeneity, there is frequently a completeness about them that makes them as much church in their own right as many parish churches. Many youth congregations are closely related to an adult partner church like the one at Threshold. Bishop Graham Cray comments,

> Youth congregations are not a bridging strategy. They are not a temporary holding camp where young people can be acclimatized to existing church. It is not a bridge to the real thing. These groups take responsibility for worship, pastoral

care, mission and evangelism. To their members they are the only real thing they know. It is an experience of the church of Jesus Christ.

In rural areas, where it is rare for there to be more than one or two young people in each church, there is huge potential for youth congregations – but frequently a lack of resources to make it happen. A solution to this may be for more deaneries or churches in the catchment areas of particular schools and colleges to work together. Sometimes youth congregations start with a youth service such as the one below and grow gradually into more of the community and mission aspects of being church.

Eden

Eden is a monthly youth service held in Steyning Grammar School in West Sussex. It is a Church of England initiative, which has been set up in the Storrington Deanery within Chichester Diocese. It evolved out of Derek Spencer's work as Storrington Deanery Youth Missioner. Since September 2001 he had been looking for ways of bringing young people together in a setting that would be Christian, credible, interactive and relevant. The main thrust of his work was, and is, done in and through local schools: the Rydon Community College in Thakesam, West Sussex, and in particular the Steyning Grammar School. The majority of young people who attend Eden have come out of the work that has been done in these schools. Early on, Derek had set up two deanery youth groups. Starting from about fifteen committed young people, these Bible and discussion groups grew until over thirty people were regularly involved.

After two years of preparation, thought and prayer, Derek gathered seven people from around the deanery to pray about the possible beginning of a youth congregation. They came up with the name 'Eden' as it reflected both a new beginning and the organic nature of the project. The first Eden service took place on 1 June 2003 and was attended by about

120 people. The feedback was very positive and there seemed to be a hunger for more of the same.

The team of seven still oversee Eden. Together, they plan and organize each of the services. Their vision and hope for the project is to create an ongoing environment, which meets the spiritual and social needs for the local young people.

Services incorporate worship; exploring the Bible; various forms of prayer; and space to respond to God. Worship is encouraged in ways that young people can relate to so that all can participate at whatever level they feel comfortable with. Behind this is a desire to recognize that all are on a journey of faith. Space before and after the 'service' is important for relationship-building, chilling out and fun. As the Edenzone website says, 'Eden is . . . Christian; Imaginative; Alternative; Multi-media; Relaxed; Participatory; Fresh . . .'.[25] The aim is to be real with God.

Traditional forms of church inspiring new interest

The point of being a mission-shaped church is not to be 'new' or 'innovative' but to be shaped by God's mission in our context. This is particularly true in the countryside where many aspects of traditional church still connect with people particularly powerfully. In a rural church, there are frequently highpoints in the year where a very large number of people want to be part of traditional church – the Carol service, Harvest, and Remembrance Sunday. At weddings, funerals and baptisms people will often say that they want them to be 'traditional'. This is seldom a plea for *The Book of Common Prayer*. Rather, it is something to do with wanting to have something that is familiar from previous experiences of church (especially hymns) and/or something to do with wanting to feel part of a tradition which has spanned the ages, with wanting the worship to have weight and depth, to experience the numinous. The 'accessible' family service, loved by some, can lack these qualities and even be highly embarrassing to others.

However, if traditional forms of church alone were the answer to our nation's spiritual malaise then our churches would be full. There is a need to look deeper – to understand our culture's spiritual hunger and which traditional forms connect with it. There is also a need for rural church to concentrate not on forms at all but on deeper values, which prove our faith authentic. The 'traditional forms of church inspiring new interest' would in the main be better described as traditional forms of worship and prayer. There are few pleas for the restoration of the traditional homily, the traditionally formal PCC meeting or traditional clerical dominance!

Simplicity in worship

One of the keys which makes some traditional worship attractive is its simplicity and space. To some, modern worship can sometimes seem busy and stage-managed. In our frenetic world people long for a little peace; time for reflection and lament as well as for thanksgiving and celebration.[26] This kind of worship can often be particularly well suited to remote rural churches.

story story story story

Tenebrae

At 9 p.m. on Good Friday, people gather at the little church of Shotesham, St Mary, for a version of the ancient service of Tenebrae. Here there is no electricity and so each one carries a candle. Three years ago, the service was attended by a handful of people. Last year the seats were full. 'Tenebrae' means shadows and in a series of nine readings and hymns or chants we in our imaginations accompany the disciples on the night of the first Good Friday as they look back over the tragic events of that day, not knowing that resurrection lies ahead. Nine more candles burn on the altar and each time the story draws a step closer to Jesus' death, one is extinguished. At last all the candles in the church are put out bar one and we wait in silence in the dark. Finally we remember 'The light shines in the darkness and the darkness has never put it out.' The service ends without a benediction and people leave, in silence, frequently in tears.

Another advantage of simple and traditional forms of worship is that they do not overtire small congregations and worship teams with resource-hungry preparations. This frees up energy and time for attractive lives of wholeness and celebration, building a loving and welcoming church community, mission and service. Such acts of worship can be led with a lighter more participative touch than perhaps they would have been in past ages, but the congregation are secure that they won't find it embarrassing or intrusive.

New monasticism

The *Faith in the Countryside* report draws attention to parallels between the rhythm of the seasons and the rhythm of disciplined prayer; between the planning of a garden and the coming of God's kingdom; between the digging of a garden and the theology of work.[27] Other aspects of an enduring rural spirituality could be seen as a celebration of creation and a connection with the land.[28] This brings with it a deeper sense of human littleness, vulnerability and dependence.[29] These traditional aspects of rural spirituality remain deeply attractive, as the popularity of the recent BBC2 series, 'The Monastery'[30] has shown, and could be seen as part of the gift which the rural church in Britain has to share with the wider society.

The growth of new monasticism can be seen as part of the recovery of traditional spiritual treasures which, while reaching into the cities, has its roots in the rhythms of nature and rural monastic life.

Northumbria Community

The seeds of the Northumbria Community were sown in the 1970s by a small group of Christians asking the key questions: 'Who is that that you seek?' and 'How then shall we live?' From their shared lives, relationships and values emerged a Rule of Availability and Vulnerability. The community is not a religious order: it consists of 'Companions' who seek to follow this Rule in their daily lives wherever they happen to live. The ethos and language of the community is strongly influenced by the heritage of the Desert Fathers and of the Celtic Saints who brought the Christian faith to Anglo-Saxon Northumbria in the seventh century.

The spirituality of this form of 'new monasticism' seeks to link the inward journey of the soul (being 'Alone' – a call to repentance and self-denial; a call to recognize and to resist evil) with the outward journey of normal life (being 'Together') to find different ways of 'being Church' ('How do we sing the Lord's song in a strange land?'). The practical means of outworking the Rule and this journey Alone/Together is through the daily rhythm of prayer (the Daily Office).

The community's mother house is the Nether Springs, situated in a beautiful quiet part of rural north Northumberland, close to Holy Island. Here, in exercising hospitality and caring for guests from all walks of life, the resident community Companions seek to share the rhythm of daily prayer with those seeking spiritual refreshment and inspiration – discovering the extraordinary in the everydayness of ordinary lives.[31]

The great variety of both ancient and new expressions of church in the countryside today is reflective of the diversity of rural life as well as its links with, and distinctiveness from, rural culture. This is a matter for celebration. However, such diversity within an institution can sometimes feel like a threat to its very identity. The next chapter therefore examines the question of whether fresh expressions ought to be identified as 'church' and indeed what it means to be Christ's Church.

5 But are fresh expressions church?

> 'It's all very well you going to cell,' said one village
> congregation member to a newer Christian, 'but why don't
> you ever go to church?'
>
> 'Oh, I go to church,' she replied, shaken but not cowed; 'The
> cell is my church.'

How can people know that the fresh expressions in which people are
increasingly participating in the countryside can be validly treated as church?
When 'church' no longer requires a parish, a vicar or a church building,
hymns or a prayer book, there is understandable confusion as to whether
'anything can be called church these days'. There is a need for values
expressing the essence of church, which can be applied to any context and
with any size of church grouping – rural or urban, a small cell or a large
minster.

The *Mission-shaped Church* report points to the four classic marks of church,
enshrined in the Nicene Creed as reminders to the Church of its true
nature and calling: We believe in one, holy catholic and apostolic
Church.

The Church's journey

These marks – being one, holy, catholic and apostolic – are presented, within
the report, as four dimensions of a journey, none of which exist without
reference to the others:

Being one is about a journey into community, expressing in practice the
unity of the Trinity and of the Body of Christ.

> A trinitarian theology of the church will speak of the oneness
> of the church ... as a differentiated oneness of distinctive
> persons-in-relation who discover their particularity in active
> relationships of giving and receiving.[1]

It is this quality in relationships which forms the basis of ecclesial unity rather than belonging to a single institution. In quality of relationships the Church is called to reflect the love that flows between the persons of the Trinity.

Being holy is about the journey towards God in worship and obedience. It must be about both seeking God himself and being transformed to be like him.

Being catholic implies that, on their journey, church communities are each connected to the Church Universal. 'The catholicity of the church is actually a mandate for cultural hospitality.'[2] Catholicity also brings a reminder that the present church is a people with a rich heritage from which to learn. George Lings points out that whereas oneness, holiness and apostolicity usually find their place in the stated values of fresh expressions of church (albeit in different terms), catholicity is sadly sometimes omitted.[3] Catholicity is important because it is a constant call to local churches to live in interdependence with other parts of the catholic Church.

Being apostolic is often seen as being about continuity between the first apostles and the Church of today. However it is as much about future direction as authorized past. The Church is 'apostolic' in that she is 'sent' by Jesus, just as the first apostles were 'sent' by him, and just as the great apostle Jesus was 'sent' by his Father. Apostolicity is about the journey outwards in mission. This mission is many faceted – proclaiming the Good News of the kingdom, teaching, baptizing and nurturing new believers, loving service; transforming unjust structures in society and caring for the creation[4] of which we are a part.

Each of these four dimensions of the journey is from Christ and for Christ. The journey is one of discipleship and each dimension involves the values expressed in his incarnation and 'dying to live'. The marks of oneness, holiness, catholicity and apostolicity remind the Church of her true nature and calling. They can therefore act as a measure for discerning how far a fresh expression has journeyed and is ready to be recognized as church.

Four dimensions of the journey in practice

In a mature mission-shaped church all four dimensions of the journey will be evident in their values and practice. The rural cell church, Threshold, described in the last chapter[5] recently produced a document reflecting on its journey over the ten years since it began.[6] It was not a document written with the four marks of church in mind, but I was fascinated to see how their practice and values had naturally taken this shape, building on the foundation of Jesus as Lord. Below I reproduce the document, slightly reordered, with comments on this example of how a fresh expression has lived out the four dimensions of being church:

Extracts from Threshold, 'The shape we are in TEN years on'

Christ as Foundation and Lord   Our foundations are:

> 1: Love for Jesus: our focus is on Jesus himself – so we seek to be a community where he is easily found – a 'place' full of the power and presence of God by his Spirit. *We seek to cooperate with the way God leads us by his Spirit.*

> 2: Love for his word as in the Bible. We value truth, integrity, and clarity about the gospel, sin and salvation. The Bible is our foundation for living. *We hold high the value of the scriptures; we have nurture, Bible teaching and preaching in place. We base our Church vision, values and practice on the Bible.*

Oneness   * Small group life is important to us especially for community building, local visibility/focus and pastoral care. *Almost all adults and youth are in cells.*

> * We focus on hospitality – we have lots of food involved in our life together especially as we live amongst our non-church friends. *Catering for large or small numbers, meals at home, Alpha suppers, special events, Sunday tea for the elderly etc.*

> * Our leadership style is collegiate, accountable to God, the people and the Network leadership. We are vision focused

and consultative, we seek to release others into their
calling and encourage them to take responsibility. *We have
an overall church leadership team of 4 leaders. We also have
leaders team for each cell, cluster, youth cell, worship, overseas
mission, children's work, etc. so that about 50 per cent of the
adults in church are involved in leading something.*

* We aim to be a safe place for the young: children and
youth are very important to us. *Approximately
40 per cent of the Church are under 20. A major area of
investment has been in employing youth workers. We have
thriving children's work and youth cells/activities.*

Holiness   * Worship and prayer are central to our life together.

* Discipleship – maturing increasingly into the likeness of Jesus
is important to us and a focus of much of our effort. *This
mostly happens through cell life as we are mutually
accountable.*

Catholicity   * We are committed to worldwide mission as God directs
us. *We have had a number of Church members involved in
overseas mission over the years. We have a team that
supports, promotes and develops overseas mission activity.*

* We seek to complement, work with and bless other
Christians and churches. Again – Kingdom, not Threshold,
first. *We actively work alongside other churches in every
community we are involved in.*

* We aim to be generous, giving away – including the release
of resources overseas to the poor and needy as well as
nearer home. *Our tithe fund is usually directed at the poor
and needy. A large portion of our budget goes toward
supporting mission activity overseas.*

Apostolicity   * Our focus is on the coming of the kingdom – our vision is
primarily to see the kingdom of God further established.
We wholeheartedly believe in the value of local church,
which arises as we seek the kingdom.

* **We live an incarnational approach – building local Christian communities within the villages/areas.** *We aim to serve our communities, to build friendship, to be visible and accessible. We have much involvement serving communities in different ways and being present in wholesome ways.*

* **We focus on relating to non-church people. Remember Psalm 84.10:'I would rather stand on the Threshold of the house of my God ...' – being part of the house of God but dwelling near the 'tents of the wicked' – so that they have easy access to the kingdom.** *We seek to be contemporary in language and culture and seek to build relationships for their own sake. This is reflected in our engagement in various communities (e.g. schools, drama groups, community groups, carnival support etc.).*

* **We have a focus on creativity: music, visual arts, drama, poetry etc.** *We have many musicians active in worship and/or bands of different kinds, several photographers, experts with video, lighting, sound reproduction, painting/sculpture and poets. We have a team committed to expressing these things in events or services.*

* **Our vision is for a wide geographical area – Lincolnshire – with a bias to the rural.**

* **Mobility and flexibility in terms of structure, meetings and working with others are important to us.**

The way Threshold lives out the four dimensions deserves some close attention. For example, I have interpreted the commitment of the church to children (who are often marginalized in rural churches) as part of the wider commitment to **oneness**. It is noteworthy that this 'oneness' built up through hospitality and small group life is sought in a way that includes rather than excludes those 'outside' the church.

Under **catholicity** I have included the church's commitment to ecumenical co-operation and also to world mission, which might be seen as part of being apostolic. It seemed to me that while it is both, it primarily belongs to the expression of the Church's catholicity because engaging in this mission is only achieved in partnership and support of the Church in other parts of the world. This may also be a more healthy way for churches to think of this aspect of their ministry – connecting with the world Church is an essential part of ecclesial identity in its own right and not an alternative to local mission.

We might notice that the sections which I've grouped under **holiness** are relatively short compared to those under **apostolicity**. I do not think that this is due to any lack of attention to worship and holiness of life. Rather, there is a sense that in those areas the Church 'knows what is doing'. On the other hand, the apostolic dimension needs constant responsiveness to the mission situation. It is interesting that this section includes quite concrete things like a commitment to arts and a bias to the rural, which show how broader values will be earthed.

The valuing of flexibility is also included under **apostolicity**. Although not obvious at first, this value is part of being a church shaped by mission, instead of letting mission be shaped by the church. In a fast-changing culture, flexibility is required in order to follow the pattern of the Incarnation and it involves 'dying to live' because of the constant need to be prepared to sacrifice ways of doing things which may have become dear. It is notable that the Bible passage that guided Threshold at the very beginning of the church-planting process is one that is central to the theology of mission-shaped church:

> 'And what you sow is not the body that is to be, but a bare seed, perhaps of wheat or some other grain. But God gives it a body as He has chosen, and to each kind of seed its own body.' (1 Corinthians 15.37-38)

Pete Atkins writes 'We had to let a seed (remnant of people) fall into the ground and let Him shape what emerged as the plant germinated. We couldn't entirely tell in advance what Threshold would look like.'[7] This is a continuing process. Threshold's 'The Shape we are in' document concludes, 'Perhaps "it does not yet appear what we shall be" but the above gives a flavour of who God has made us at present.'

Beginning the journey in different places

George Lings notes that 'a community following the dynamic balance of these ... journeys may find different ones have greater emphasis at different points in the story.'[8] In the past traditional church planting has most often started with worship services. Of the four marks of church above, this could be seen as being most closely related to the mark of 'being holy'. Worship is still a valid beginning for a fresh expression of church as in the story of Eden.[9] However today church plants and fresh expressions often need to begin with other aspects of the journey.

One example of a fresh expression of church which deliberately chose not to start with worship is an initiative started in June 2005 by St Mary's Church, Haddenham, in the Diocese of Oxford. Coordinator of the new venture, Tim Shaw, writes

> We realized that our predominant activity ... was to hold a service of worship – a presentational religious event ... We have recognized that we now live in a post-Christian society and if we want to connect with this culture, the provision of a worship service as the main activity when we gather together is not the right starting-point. Although worship must be an essential part of our church life, the Caféplus+ vision is to provide a more neutral setting for enquirers to experience other aspects of church such as celebration, fellowship, sharing food, prayer and community.[10]

The background to the development of the new vision was that the church were aware that they were no longer engaging with the local village community in as culturally relevant way as they would wish and that the congregation was haemorrhaging people of the younger generation. Their village community is a relatively large one – 6,000 inhabitants with a strong village identity – and this offered certain opportunities.

Caféplus+

Caféplus+ is a breakfast café, running from
9.30 a.m. to 12.30 p.m. on the first Sunday of each month
with high quality, fresh coffee, tea, continental breakfast and
newspapers, all provided free by the church. Other things
happen during the morning depending on the resources
available and using the various rooms of the village hall venue.
There is a crèche in a space adjacent to the café and a
children's Sunday school running in another room for part of
the morning. In a third room, there is a Quiet Space and the
opportunity for prayer ministry. Each month there will be
different one-off events of general interest to the community:
a litter-picking party round the village, a demonstration by
hand bell ringers, a craft sale for a Third World charity.
A presentation called 'Food 4 Thought' takes place at 10.30
a.m. – presenting contemporary issues from a Christian
perspective with an emphasis on accessibility and informality.

Caféplus+ is still developing. There are hopes to offer an
enquirers' course as an optional activity in part of the venue
in the future and from this there could grow cells and
worship.[11] It may eventually develop into a church in its
own right.

Direction in the journey

All expressions of church are partial. The four marks of church can help us
in seeing what can be validated as church but they are also a 'model for
health'[12] to inspire parishes as well as fresh expressions. The key thing is
direction in the journey. Is the church seeking to follow Christ in being one,
holy, catholic and apostolic? This can be a call to repentance for churches
who have neglected one of the dimensions of the journey. If a church
community is no longer able or willing to make this journey, whether it has
been established for two weeks or a thousand years, it may be that it has
ceased to be a church – certainly, it is not a 'mission-shaped' church.

Not all initiatives which have been called 'fresh expressions' are church in themselves. Some are on the journey to becoming church. Others are really mission initiatives that are part of the life of a church. For example, David Clayden describes the café church in Thorndon as a 'Bridge meeting' point for people to 'taste' church without feeling any pressure to conform. Moving into fuller discipleship requires moving beyond the café church into other strands of local church life. Many of those who go have started attending Family Worship or Morning Prayer on other Sundays too. Some have gone forward for confirmation. To say something is a 'mission initiative', rather than a 'fresh expression of church/church plant' is not to downgrade it. Both are good and important. However, making the distinction between the two is important because this tells us about the vision for the future. A mission initiative will develop as part of existing church structures, contributing to the expression of the four marks of church within the whole. Good mission initiatives will nevertheless be a challenge to the existing church which, if healthy, will find itself reshaped by its participation in that mission. Fresh expressions of church seek to grow the four marks of church within themselves. They also need to work from dependence towards a degree of independence and interdependence from the planting church.

Helping churches to grow up – the 'three self' principles[13]

The great nineteenth-century missionary Henry Venn was one of the first people to campaign for indigenous churches that belonged to the culture of the people and were led by local people. He put forward the idea that these new churches needed to move from dependence on mother church to being self-financing, self-governing and self-propagating. These 'three self' principles have been developed and are now taken for granted as good practice in missionary situations. This section looks at the meaning of these principles and how rural fresh expressions can be helped to meet these challenges to grow to maturity.

Self-financing

Learning to pay their own way is vital to the discipleship growth of those who are church members of both fresh expressions and parish churches.

We pay for what we value and it helps members to recognize that their church family is precious. This stewardship is not the same as learning Christian giving – responding to the overwhelming generosity of God by giving freely – but it is a step along the way. Dioceses can help by helping parishes and fresh expressions to know exactly what the cost of the actual ministry they receive is so that they can work towards paying their way.

The parish share system can be applied in ways that either help or hinder growth towards being self-financing. If the total costs of the diocese are simply divided according to a formula, fresh expressions cannot learn to take responsibility for their own costs. Like many parish churches, they may even see the levy as an unreasonable demand by which they are subsidising others – even when it is actually they who are receiving the subsidy. The principle of sharing our resources according to need across the diocese needs to be accompanied by accurate figures about the actual costs for each church, fresh expression or each multi-parish benefice. In this way those who are being subsidized can plan towards being self-financing and those churches whose giving subsidizes others can learn of the ministry that they enable to happen and be encouraged in this practical expression of catholicity.

For church plants and fresh expressions of church, paying their way (especially through parish share contributions) is one of the major ways in which they gain recognition from older forms of church.

Self-governing

All churches learn responsibility from running their own affairs. Making decisions and learning from mistakes (and successes) are an essential part of growing up. Self-governance doesn't mean a lack of connection with other churches which, as we have seen, are essential to catholicity. Rather, it is a case of moving from a dependent relationship to a more equal partnership. In my own benefice, we are being encouraged by the diocese to experiment with forms of governance for the cell church with a view to it eventually gaining something equivalent to parish status.

The importance of the blessing and guidance of bishops and senior staff can hardly be overstated in the growth of fresh expressions to maturity. There is no Anglican fresh expression in this book that has flourished and grown over a long period without the active interest and support of a local bishop. The role of the bishop is particularly key in giving permission for fresh expressions to learn a degree of self-governance, at this time when the legal frameworks to make this normative are still not in place.

A lack of legal status makes fresh expressions of church particularly vulnerable to changes in clergy and gives them no say in appointments. It also gives them no appropriate representation at deanery, diocesan or national level. Among the new legal frameworks which are being developed some are needed which will enable the 'mixed economy' to become a fully recognized reality within multi-parish benefices and other rural structures for ministry. At present, there is no way of giving a network church in the cure of the incumbent of a multi-parish benefice or team equivalent status to the PCCs unless it has a geographical base. It is important that the mission of these mission-shaped churches is not distorted by the need to fit in with current models designed for other circumstances.

Self-propagating

To be self-propagating is to be able to plant new churches. In a rural area, examples of this might be sending a team to help in a nearby parish or by the multiplication of cells. Key to this is the development of maturity in discipleship and a variety of ministries including leadership. This is an area in which fresh expressions naturally excel and new training courses provided regionally or nationally will help in the ministerial formation of mission pioneers.

Fresh expressions – on the way

The development of the 'three self' principles is well underway in the Cherwell Valley Fresh Expressions described in Chapter 4. Supported by Oxford Diocese, Church Army officer Ian Biscoe, who planted the church together with his wife Erika, has had to modify his role from pioneer evangelist to making disciples and structural development of the young church.

Self-financing – The four new congregations are about to make their first contribution towards parish share.

Self-governing – A leaders/elders cell has emerged to take on similar responsibilities to a PCC. Ian himself is spending part of his time training for ordination under the new 'pioneer minister' category. Now the church plant has become part of a multi-parish team ministry, part of the work to be done in the next few years is to work out appropriate structures to give legal status alongside the existing PCCs.

Self-propagating – The four congregations, which have developed over the last four years, are now largely led by the new members of the church and Cherwell Valley Fresh Expressions continues to grow.

For fresh expressions to grow to maturity and bear fruit, we need a generation of lay leaders, clergy and bishops who are able to work with the whole of the 'mixed economy'. This will be especially key in rural areas where fresh expressions and parish churches need to co-operate closely together and the same person may have pastoral oversight of both. This is a responsibility not only for individual parish churches and fresh expressions to develop but also a responsibility for the national church and training institutions as they play their part in formation for ministry. As Bishop Graham James has said,

> We badly need clergy with the flexibility to be, as St Paul puts it, 'all things to all people for the sake of the gospel'. They need to have an intelligent appreciation of the parochial system. They need to speak different languages. They need a sound understanding of contemporary society and an ability to offer a theological critique. They'll need that theology to survive. They'll need a bit more than a few new ways of being church. They'll need to be able to be used themselves in new ways.[14]

6 Pruning the vine – restructuring rural church for mission

In Autumn 2005, one of our Sunday schools returned from a trip to the Tas Valley vineyard. The enthusiasm of the farmer had communicated itself to them and they eagerly poured out to me and the startled congregation the importance of pruning vines. Apparently vines grow too many leaves, making a tangled mess which blocks out the light. They need to be pruned to let the sun in and so they can focus their energy on producing good quality grapes. This is the familiar image Jesus uses in John 15 to teach about the future of God's people: 'I am the True Vine and my Father is the Vinedresser. He removes every branch in me that does not bear fruit and he prunes every branch that does bear fruit, so it will be clean and bear more fruit' (John 15.1-2).

The disciples have 'already been pruned' by the 'word' Jesus has spoken to them (John 15.3), calling them to pick up their cross and follow him (Matthew 16.24; Mark 8.34; 10.21; Luke 9.23). However, in this farewell discourse Jesus hints at ongoing pruning to come. The Spirit's call to mission beyond the Jews was to lead to Gentile believers and to the decision that circumcision and food laws should not apply to them. This in turn led to persecution and the separation of the church from the Jewish nation. The pruning was so radical that God's people could no longer be simply identified with the nation of Israel. The vine becomes Christ – his people. Paul talks of the Gentile church as a graft onto the old root stock.[1] This pruning was terribly painful but it was also the necessary precursor to ongoing fruit in the Gentile world.

Pruning and 'dying to live'

No book on mission-shaped church would be complete without reflecting on both the pruning which is necessary at a local and a national level for the sake of mission. Pruning continues throughout the life of a vine – and as part of God's vine, the rural church is not exempt from the vinedresser's knife.

It is part of the spiritual dynamic of 'dying to live'.[2] This chapter contains a plea to reflect seriously on some contentious issues, first of all in local pruning and secondly nationally in considering the careful, selective pruning of structures and buildings:

> Though it always hurts, we must be ready for the father's pruning knife. God is glorified, and so will we be, by bearing good quality fruit, and lots of it. For that to happen, there will be extra growth that needs cutting away. That too is an intimate process. The vine-dresser is never closer to the vine, taking more thought over its long term health and productivity than when he has the knife in his hand.[3]

Local pruning

One example of courageous pruning which is beginning to bear fruit is that of the beginning of Caféplus+ in Haddenham whose story was told in Chapter 5.

story story story story

Caféplus+

One of the most difficult decisions to make in the planning stage of Caféplus+ was whether to continue holding the morning service in church concurrently. Giving this up was a real sacrifice, but keeping both going involved spreading resources too thinly. The pruning enabled the whole church to own that this expression of outreach and celebration was an essential part of the identity of St Mary's rather than an add-on for those 'keen on that sort of thing'.

Today, about 180 people attend the breakfast café each month, a third of whom don't usually come to church. The Vicar, Chris Denham, comments, 'We have all been amazed at how easy it is to engage newcomers in conversations in this café setting. I have also noted with satisfaction that Caféplus+ is fully engaging and helping to retain the younger generation.'

> By pruning a morning service, St Mary's members have already created a church activity to which they can invite friends in the genuine belief that they will love it. Further fruit will come if this (as seems likely) leads to the growth of discipleship and a more truly inculturated form of church.

Many rural congregations are much smaller than the one in Haddenham and the sacrifices to be made will seem even greater. When the church roof is falling in and the congregation numbers less than twenty, to spend time and effort sharing the gospel authentically with people who will never financially support the church building is a real sacrifice. However, if this is what a church or group of rural churches feels God has called them to, this is a sacrifice that can be made with joy. Pruning enables the growth of fresh shoots. We are not only called to dying – after death comes resurrection – we are dying to live.

Pruning is not only vital for fresh expressions. It is vital for all churches at whatever stage of maturity and at every level. At national and diocesan level too, the Church is learning to travel lighter in order to make more space and release gifts and energy for mission. The *Mission-shaped Church* report draws particular attention to two areas which require urgent consideration for the sake of mission in the countryside: church buildings and the structure of the multi-parish benefice. These are complex areas fraught with contentious issues – and careful, prayerful, discerning pruning is needed; but it cannot be left too much longer for the tangled mess is already cutting out the light: 'Unless the Church of England willingly sacrifices the wrong things, it may end up unwillingly sacrificing the right ones.'[4]

Shrines and slide rules – towards a mission perspective on church buildings

One of the greatest challenges facing the rural church is how to accommodate the assumptions and expectations of the modern citizen in terms of providing even the most basic of amenities, without compromising the serious business of

sacred space working God's will on hearts and minds in
retreat from urban cynicism and secularization.[5]

In my own Diocese of Norwich there are around 650 church buildings. This
is more per acre and per person than anywhere else in the world. Most are
medieval; listed Grade I or II*.[6] Church buildings can be beautiful and
inspirational. They stand as a witness within the rural landscape. Rural people
are frequently deeply attached to them, not only as spiritual places, but as
places of the memory of family weddings and baptisms, the location of the
family graves and as the most distinctive historical landmark of the village.
What a resource for mission!

On the other hand, the report of a working party of the Norwich Diocese
reflects that church buildings are not an unmitigated blessing. Entitled *Church
Buildings: A Source of Delight and a Cause of Anxiety*,[7] the report reflects both
the creative use of church buildings and the heartache over repairs and the
need for facilities:

> In addition, many of the growing churches we have looked at
> so far, are thriving without such a historic resource or have
> perceived a need to move outside their church building for
> the purposes of mission. Anecdotal evidence as well as
> common sense suggests that churches which meet in warm
> low-cost, low-maintenance accommodation with access to
> toilets and kitchen are more likely to grow. In a rural multi-
> parish benefice, the sheer numbers of wonderful historic
> buildings without such facilities can be overwhelming.

Church buildings as shrines

A way to understand the function that church buildings can play in
nourishing Christian community is offered by John Inge in his acclaimed
book, *A Christian Theology of Place*.[8] He uses the model of pilgrimage, with
the 'shrine' as the destination or staging post in pilgrimage.[9] Pilgrimage has a
very important place in Christian tradition. Firstly, it reminds us of our roots
– the heritage of which we are a part as Christian people. Secondly, the
journey reminds us that our whole lives are about journeying into and with

God. Thirdly, the destination of a pilgrimage speaks to us sacramentally of our ultimate destination – the consummation of all things in Christ:[10]

> Viewing all our churches[11] as shrines and using them as such would have a profoundly positive effect upon the witness of the Christian Church. Should not all churches be places where there is a history of divine self communication, of 'sacramental encounters' with the worshipping community that inhabits them? Should not their presence in that community nourish the faith of that community? Should they not proclaim to the secular world in which they stand that God is present and active in this world? Cannot each journey made to such a church be thought of as a 'mini-pilgrimage'?[12]

The idea of the church building as a shrine is extraordinarily helpful in understanding the place such buildings have in the hearts of some parishioners. Pilgrimage and sacred space have an important felt place in popular contemporary spirituality. Many church tourists report feeling that ancient church buildings are spiritual places[13] – and that may be particularly true of remote churches. The recently formed Small Pilgrim Places Network[14] supports a network of places of quiet prayer, which are typically churches. Larger rural shrines such as that of our Lady at Walsingham also continue to have popular appeal. A shrine is a place that a person might visit quite seldom, but has great emotional importance. People might also feel quite strongly that some changes should not be made to a shrine.

Church buildings as home for Christian community

Church members do not always see themselves as guardians of a shrine, even though Inge suggests that they should. This is particularly true of those from a Nonconformist background who are equal and often key members of Anglican churches in rural areas. For them, the church building is primarily the home of the Christian community[15] and this requires quite different qualities and facilities. In rural dioceses, as many as 50 per cent of the schemes considered by the Advisory Committee for the Care of Churches can relate to the provision of toilets and kitchens. Many other applications relate to heating. John Saxbee suggests that where such aspirations cannot be met within the parish church, 'consideration must be given to licensing alternative centres of parish worship, thus releasing the ancient buildings to do what they do best, witnessing to God's enduring presence at the heart of rural culture and community'.[16]

There are a number of reasons why the dual functions of the rural parish church as shrine and community building, always in tension with each other, may in individual cases reach a point where they ought to be separated:

- Conservation issues may prevent the building being adapted to the needs of contemporary church communities, especially when the building is listed.

- The financial cost of maintaining or altering the building may not be the potentially most fruitful use of resources which could be used in other forms of mission, especially in areas where there is a high number of buildings in proportion to the size of population. At present the costs of maintaining church buildings are rising much faster than inflation due to factors beyond the control of PCCs: Health and Safety legislation and the Disability Discrimination Act require a significantly higher standard of safety and accessibility than was envisaged when these buildings were built and make adaptation necessary.[17] At the same time, adaptation has become more difficult and expensive due to higher standards of materials and workmanship required by heritage bodies and a shortage of skilled labour. Grant aid is about half of what it was in 1995 when measured in real terms.

- There may be insufficient members of the local church community who feel that the tending of the building and the attendant fundraising is a ministry that they are able to undertake. At the same time, the potential burden of this task acts as a deterrent to some who might otherwise join the church.

When this happens, at present, there are few options. If a PCC no longer needs its building and/or cannot afford to maintain it, there are few other church organizations which will care for it as a holy place. In most rural places, if the building does not function as the home of the congregation it can no longer function as a shrine. In some cases, the importance of the building to the village is such that villagers will go beyond protesting at proposed redundancy and be willing to actively share in responsibility for the building. Here is an idea that we are exploring in one of the small villages in the Tas Valley.

story
story
story
story

Local trust ownership

It may be possible for the Church Commissioners to transfer ownership of the parish church to a charitable trust set up by villagers which will be responsible for the building and churchyard, alterations, maintenance, repair and running costs. The aim is that the current building would be sympathetically adapted for wider community use while retaining its use as a place of Christian worship.

In our case, the building itself is suitable as both 'shrine' and 'community building', but the core congregation is very small and mainly older people and is likely to struggle to maintain the building in the future unless creative action is taken. The scheme, if successful, is in many ways going back to a more medieval pattern of use for the building – reflecting the belief that 'there is nothing in human life in which God is not already involved'.[18] It would secure for the village an attractive venue for a wide range of community activities conveniently situated near the playing field and the long-term future of the most outstanding landmark of the village, the social history represented in the fabric of the structure and a quiet place for prayer. The trust would also ensure the continuance of the church as a place of Christian worship, and written into the deeds of the building and accompanying land would be an undertaking that the use of the building would always reflect Christian principles. Similarly, the trust would continue to grant to parishioners the right to be buried in the churchyard. A representative of the incumbent or PCC would be on the board of trustees and the Bishop of Norwich would license it as a parish centre of worship so that all the services which take place in a parish church could continue there.

The scheme, if successful, would also help the church community to become more 'mission-shaped': instead of being a gracious provider, on our own terms (in Christendom mode), we would become a partner and stake-holder. The building which is home to us could be alive through consistent use and become a shared home, not just rented out, to a variety of ways of expressing village life. This would increase the possibility of overlaps between the Christian and village community and could decrease the barriers in crossing between the two. As we continue to use the building for worship, the improved heating, toilets and access, together with release from the responsibility of maintaining the building, might help us to rebuild our congregation but our influence would have to be by quality not power.[19]

It is true to say that many rural church buildings, which are seen as problematic, could be used more creatively. Less than half of rural parish churches are used for activities other than Sunday worship:[20] 'Church buildings have ceased by and large to speak clearly of a present reality, and instead convey a mumbled message of a glorious though faded past.'[21]

There are many examples within this book alone of church buildings being used well for community purposes. A level playing field with secular organizations in access to resources to develop community services within church buildings is much needed and would make more of these buildings usable for mission.[22] Nevertheless, even this will not provide the whole answer. If rural churches have little time or energy left for anything other than the building, they will be, as Bob Jackson warns, 'crushed by' their 'own heritage'.[23] There is a need to consider which buildings serve the purposes of mission and ministry and which actually act as a block. However, in some quarters questions about whether God is calling us to close any of our parish churches are almost taboo. Why has this happened?

Church buildings as transitional objects

One of the reasons why Church of England members find it difficult to contemplate the closure of any parish church buildings is that, emotionally speaking, they feel as if the identity and future of the church itself rested on them. In psychosocial terms these buildings could be described as 'transitional objects'.[24] Most of as children had a favourite teddy, doll or blanket from which we were virtually inseparable. This 'transitional object' was very important in that it helped us to move from an infant's view of almost complete identity with our world to one where we were able to make distinctions between ourselves and others. However, if the object was taken away to be washed, we were distraught – so closely did we identify with it that we felt our very existence was threatened in some way.

Although we outgrow our soft toys, all adults continue to have more sophisticated 'transitional objects or phenomena' – valued possessions, skills or experiences which we identify with closely and which reassure us about who we are and our place in the world. While these usually have a positive role in helping adults to function, on occasion such 'transitional phenomena' may become a fixation which make it difficult for the people involved to deal with the changing nature of their surroundings. This concept has been developed to show how the unconscious significance of transitional objects can lead to resistance to change in the life of organizations and communities. The general principles are well illustrated by the case study below:

Hanging on to the slide rules

An engineering company ... experienced difficulties in adapting to changes being created by new developments in computer technology. One of the interesting features of the culture of the company was its commitment to the use of slide rules. While the new computer technology ... offered a more efficient way of making engineering calculations, many of the engineers insisted on continuing to use their 'slides'. The theory of transitional phenomena leads us to understand this in terms of an unconscious process where the use of slide rules was associated with a past that was fast disappearing and a reluctance to relinquish an old identity. As might be expected, the firm lost their position in the industry and eventually got taken over by another firm.[25]

As a Church, we are an organization coping with massive amounts of societal change and so the monuments in stone, which recall past glories and enduring worship down the ages, acquire an even greater symbolic importance. Transitional theory would suggest that unwillingness to close buildings even when they no longer effectively serve the church community's mission arises because the buildings have become transitional phenomena in which members have invested their sense of identity. Change will only occur when people have had time and space for exploration of what their identity as church is so that they are prepared to relinquish what they hold dear for the sake of acquiring something new. Fresh expressions of church are helpful here for they help the wider Church of England to imagine what a church community might look like without a building and to find new ways of thinking about ecclesial identity.

Financial barriers

A second reason why we often continue using our buildings even when they cease to facilitate the purposes of worship and mission is financial. Dioceses may discourage churches from making their buildings redundant partly because the cost of the care of those buildings would then fall to the dioceses themselves. Only about half of the church buildings made redundant since 1969 have been able to be sold for residential, business or community or other uses. In addition, the Churches Conservation Trust, financed jointly by Church and State, cares for about a fifth of redundant churches but with flat funding from Government only very few buildings can now be passed into its care. If neither of these options is available the diocese must care for the building itself or have it demolished. The consequence is that a number of diocesan bishops will not permit a parish to have a building made redundant, even if that building is a ruin and completely unusable for worship or church community use, unless an alternative use is found first.

The difficulty of making a ruin redundant illustrates very powerfully that church structures are a long way from being mission-shaped in the area of buildings. In one rural diocese, I understand that there are around 150 ruins being cared for by parish churches. Members of PCCs are liable if these sites are not kept safe. Conservation factors frequently prevent the use of the land for other purposes. Thousands of pounds and countless hours are spent by small rural church communities dutifully caring for the sites of ruins that are seldom in any way a resource for mission.

I would suggest that becoming a mission-shaped church in the countryside will require us to address this issue by taking more redundant buildings and ruins into the care of the national or diocesan Church. One important reason for this is pastoral: I will never forget visiting one country church building and meeting the elderly churchwarden. He was clearly distressed as he told me how he felt it was his duty to carry on alone because there was no one else. He realized the legal and practical duties of warden were beyond him. As the benefice was in interregnum, he had asked the bishop for help but had been strongly encouraged to continue as long as possible. Dioceses need to consider at what stage encouragement to carry on with weighty responsibilities is unreasonable or even becomes abusive.

Secondly, it is clear that, by leaving ruins and unused 'mothballed' buildings at parish level, the scale of the issue has been hidden and no effective action has been taken. If such buildings were held at a higher level, the Church as a whole would be shocked at the scale of the problem. This would result in a higher priority being given to persuading the state that if the law requires preservation of buildings, the state must take financial responsibility, whenever this makes the site unusable:

> Churches in the countryside struggle to subsidize the conservation of the nation's heritage to the extent that they have in past years. It is important that they are able to consider first the mission to which God has called them.[26]

Finding a new starting-point

It is essential to a mission-shaped church that it is allowed to ask not only how but also whether its buildings are to be used. The model of church building as shrine suggests in itself the need for this question. The great holy place of the biblical story, the Temple in Jerusalem, is only a staging post for heaven – and for long periods of history, God took his people into exile even from that shrine in order that they might find him afresh. As well as the Temple, we have much to learn from the exile and the time of wandering in the desert.[27] Perhaps the Church, as God's pilgrim people of this day, also needs to learn to 'pitch the tent' of God's presence and have a lighter attachment to buildings.

If the Church of England in the countryside is to become a mission-shaped church, it is essential to stop using the church buildings as if they were a unalterable starting point. Beginning with questions like, 'How can we get people to come to our church?' or 'How can we use our church building for mission?' prejudges the answer as to how we engage in mission so that the current buildings and structures provide the limits and the shape that Christian mission can take. Church communities need to be freed to discover the part of God's mission to which each is called so that it becomes God's mission which limits and shapes their choices about how and whether to use church buildings.

Parochial structure – a healthy cure?

The multi-parish benefice

The 'multi-parish benefice' is the predominant pattern of rural ministry in the Church of England today. The pattern largely arose in response to the national need to redistribute clergy from rural areas to urban areas – especially with the arrival of the Sheffield formula in 1974.[28] In my own benefice, each of the six villages had a rector of their own within living memory. There is now one full time and one half time priest – a quarter of the number of clergy while the population has grown. Because rural parishes have relatively small populations they have been joined together to share an incumbent, but the various parish churches retain separate parochial church councils and electoral rolls.

Nobody would claim that multi-parish benefices were designed with mission in mind, but they have their advantages: there is a fond remembrance of what the vicar used to do, together with an awareness that clergy today are more thinly spread and cannot do it all. At best, this results in each church community feeling a strong responsibility for mission and pastoral care within their own parish. Secondly, in a happy multi-parish benefice, there will be a valuing of each other's different styles and an appreciation that while each small church has not got the resources to touch all the different cultures, needs and preferences in their own parish, across the benefice it is possible to develop a variety of mission initiatives and styles of worship. If local church members have already experienced that their church is in creative partnership with other churches in the benefice, starting a fresh expression of church with new Christians who do not find it easy to relate to the existing congregations can seem like the most natural thing in the world. It would be a partner in the gospel with a mission which complements the group or team.[29]

However, the very structures of a multi-parish benefice are cumbersome and easily act as a brake to mission. Imagine six or more annual meetings in the Easter period. Imagine having to take the issue of the distribution of the benefice share among the parishes to six PCC meetings. Any one council refusing to agree to a formula starts the process all over again. Just as you have got agreement a major donor to a smaller church dies or moves away and that PCC's income is halved so they are still unable to pay their share and negotiations start again with all the other PCCs. Imagine the decisions over the benefice youth group, the pattern of services, clergy expenses and shared mission work needing to go through the same process of visiting each PCC. Imagine that for a total congregation of 120 you need to apply for 3 different copyright licenses, 7 lots of buildings insurance and find 6 treasurers, 14 churchwardens and 7 fabric officers able to cope with complicated grant applications. If you are the incumbent of a multi-parish benefice, you will not have to imagine these things. This will be just be everyday reality.

Of course, it is true that with good will the multi-parish benefice becomes much easier to manage. In our team, the PCCs delegate many decisions to the quarterly Warden's meeting which helps a great deal. However, in the best of benefices, there will always be times when PCCs will take different views and this can produce deadlock. Naturally, the areas in which this may take place are the very ones which PCCs are reluctant to delegate to a Joint PCC or Team council. The multi-parish benefice also leads to a multiplication of meetings and form filling for the incumbent. In small communities, vital functions such as 'treasurer' or 'churchwarden' may be reluctantly filled by someone ill-suited for the task because nobody else is available. Some rural incumbents even find themselves doing the books. This is not a good use of our resources for mission.

In addition, it may be more difficult for network-based fresh expressions to grow to maturity in the multi-parish benefice context, because when each parish church has its own PCC, an initiative which crosses the whole benefice and does not belong to a single PCC fresh expressions of church will not have a suitable mechanism for accountability. Even in cases where there is a Joint PCC,[30] it is difficult for a fresh expression to find an equal place alongside older forms of church. It will have no structures equivalent to that of the parish churches, even if it is numerically much larger than many of the parish churches.

Generally, a more sympathetic structure for a mission-shaped church, within the current possibilities, would be that of a single parish with either informal subgroups or DCCs[31] for each parish church or fresh expression. This is not an option that many PCCs consider because they fear that they will lose their building, their funds or their control over local worship styles. Such fears are largely unfounded. A single parish may have any number of parish churches and allows great flexibility as to what is kept at the level of each church community within it and what is shared, and in particular would allow roles which require a degree of expertise to be shared by a number of churches when desirable.

There needs to be real encouragement for PCCS of small parishes to take this option seriously and to understand the burden that a multi-parish benefice structure places on lay and ordained ministry within their own village. However, one size is unlikely to fit all and a variety of models for ministry needs to be encouraged. In many places, a larger church in the benefice may have a special relationship with smaller ones, resourcing and enabling training and mission. In others, it may be appropriate to reduce the number of PCCs from 6 to 8 to 2 or 3, grouping parishes in units which can work effectively together in mission.

Yes minster?

In his book *Parochial Vision: The future of the English parish*,[32] Nick Spencer writes of a need to think again about the parish as the unit for ministry. He calls for a rediscovery of the role of the minster that played its part in the evangelization of Britain in the seventh and eighth centuries. John Finney also sees the minster community as well suited to engage in mission in a context where many seek God outside traditional church structures.[33]

Anglo-Saxon minsters were based on monastries and as such were both centres of communal life and bases for evangelism. The need for such resourcing from a strong local centre and for countering clergy isolation makes this model very attractive for the present day. It is not surprising that there has been much thought about whether all deaneries in rural areas should operate as minsters based on market towns. The difficulties arise in the compatibility of many benefices in deaneries. Often their incumbents and other ministers will have quite different theologies and consequently different visions for mission. As in team ministries, imposed collaboration where vision is not shared is likely to prove a recipe for disaster. Energies are used up in trying to make the team work instead of outwardly in mission. However, there is a quasi-minster pattern which seems to be evolving quite naturally: some larger churches are becoming resource churches linked to a network of smaller churches who share their particular vision. For example, Holy Trinity, Brompton, is as about as far from being a rural church as it is possible to get – but as the home of the *Alpha* course, run in many rural areas, and as a centre of resourcing, training and fellowship, it has some elements of being a sort of minster to many hundreds of rural churches.

Rural churches often choose to be linked with something that provides the role of a minister in providing resourcing and partnership in mission, training, prayer and encouragement. This could be a larger rural church locally, a place of pilgrimage like Walsingham or it might be an urban church or even a network such as Cell Church UK or New Wine.

Creating expectations of flexibility

Generally speaking, all new patterns of ministry need to be grown up from below and the process of legal change made simpler to understand and quicker to execute. An expectation needs to be created that the number of parishes within the multi-parish benefice can be changed according to mission need. One way to do this would for all multi-parish benefices to go through a supported process of reflection and reassessment of the most appropriate structures for their area at every interregnum. Much thinking has been done nationally about lightening the structures in urban areas to accommodate innovative church models. This is even more vital in rural areas, where the structures do not only prohibit innovation but are excessively burdensome for the size of existing small village churches to flourish.

The challenge ahead

The Church of England in the countryside is still reeling from radical pruning in terms of clergy numbers but it seems that this has left us with a lopsided plant and we need to prune in other areas. In our many small parishes with many buildings and small congregations we have a lot of bushy growth and some fruit. The pastoral system of parishes was developed at a time when people spent their working and leisure time within their own village. Church buildings were largely constructed for the needs of the medieval period and are not always suited to their purpose in the twenty-first century. Where the structures of the rural church are shaped for twenty-first-century mission it tends to be as much by happy accident as by current design. A failure to prune at national, diocesan and local level will severely hamper the health of the vine and its ability to bear fruit.

7 Together for the harvest

This chapter seeks to dispel some stereotypes and indicate how synergy can be created with traditional forms of church working alongside fresh expressions in rural mission. Finally, it considers the nature of reaping and keeping God's harvest in the countryside.

New wine – old wine skins?

'New wine, old wine skins' was the title of a seminar I was asked to give at a recent mission conference.[1] Being unused to receiving invitations like this, I was flattered and foolish enough to accept without thinking too deeply. Only afterwards did I look at the subtitle on the brochure: 'Is new life possible for dying Christian communities, or should they be allowed to rest in peace while we wait for something new?' I suddenly realized that the given title was based on a common misconception: 'No one puts new wine into old wineskins; otherwise the new wine will burst the skins and will be spilled and the skins will be destroyed. but new wine must be put into fresh wineskins' (Luke 5.37-38, NRSV).

I love being with church planters and fresh expressions enthusiasts. I love their passion, their enthusiasm and their creativity. However, there can sometimes be an unhelpful slipping into an assumption that only new style 'successful' churches can know the 'new wine' of the kingdom while more traditional churches must be 'dead'. This view doesn't fit either the experience of rural church or the theology of the Bible.

People who have invested much in an older or more traditional way of doing things are always going to find innovation uncomfortable. However, Jesus was not talking about every new idea that God's people might have. Rather, he is talking about the particular new thing he is bringing – the new wine of the kingdom of God (Jeremiah 31.12; Joel 2.19, 24); the new wine still experienced by all who follow Christ. The 'new wine' of the kingdom is often seen in rural churches most clearly in those who have faithfully followed Christ over many years and whose faith has been nurtured by traditional forms. 'New wine' is not about new ways *per se*; it is about the transforming grace by which God makes us new. This is well-illustrated by this wonderful story, told by Ann Morisey in her book *Journeying Out*:

A cascade of grace

At a Mothers' Union meeting at a village in Kent, the speakers were three Mothers' Union workers from Zimbabwe. In their presentation they spoke of how important hand-sewing machines were to the villages in Zimbabwe where there was no electricity. The word went round and soon there were eight old sewing machines retrieved from peoples' lofts and cellars. However, the Zimbabwean women advised that the only way they could reliably reach the villages would be if they were delivered personally.

The British women, all over 60, were faced with a challenge – would they organize a few jumble sales to pay the shipping costs only to have the machines moulder in a customs yard, or would they go to Zimbabwe themselves and carry the sewing machines to the villages? Would they choose venturesome love? ... They chose:

- The local newspaper followed the women's story at every stage, carrying the implicit message that church involvement does not have to be dull and predictable.

- The family of each woman hotly debated whether their mother was being reckless in taking such risks ... especially with her bad back. The grandchildren, however, thought that their grandmother was cool.

- Prayer became passionate.

- An understanding of world-development issues grew.

- The women were transformed by their experience ...

> • An ongoing relationship was created between villagers in
>   Kent and villagers in Zimbabwe.
>
> …The cascade of grace is so overflowing that it cannot be
> tracked.[2]

Jesus' 'new wine' will make churches mission-shaped – but it will not
necessarily make them look trendy or make them fit in with our assumptions
about what 'fresh expressions' should look like. Jesus' new wine will make
churches mission-shaped because they are drawn into participating in the
mission of God, which is a bigger thing altogether.

What then is the application of the warning about 'old wineskins' in our
context? In Jesus' day, old wineskins could not be used for fermenting new
wine because the leather had already been fully stretched and could not
accommodate the fermenting process without risking them bursting. 'Old
wineskins' occur where our rules and structures and preconceived ideas can
no longer stretch to accommodate the wine of the kingdom as it ferments
in our midst. As we think about mission-shaped church, there is a warning
here both for traditionalists and innovators for no human being is exempt
from the temptation to confuse their preferred style of church with the new
wine of kingdom life. The challenge for the Church of England at this
moment in history is articulated by Archbishop Rowan Williams:

> How does the church organize itself in such a way that a) it
> doesn't simply send out the message that fresh expressions,
> new encounters are a kind of tolerable eccentricity on the
> edge? b) but neither does it send out the message that
> everything people are doing as the moment is wrong and
> they need to forget it?[3]

The future of the mixed economy

Being a mission-shaped church with a 'mixed economy' means recognizing
the 'new wine' wherever it occurs and seeking to supply new flexible
structures – wineskins which can stretch as forms of church develop and
grow. The assurance that the new wine of the kingdom flows through both

traditional and fresh expressions of church is not to make any kind of judgement about the models of church that may prevail in rural areas in the future. Questions have been asked about whether the national Church is anticipating 'the Heineken effect' (refreshes the parts other churches don't reach) or 'the Orange effect' (the future is bright, the future is Orange) as the door is opened to fresh expressions.[4] As far as the countryside is concerned, 'the Heineken effect' is already here – fresh expressions are reaching parts of the rural scene which are no longer touched by the parish churches. However, it is unclear whether 'the Orange effect' will ever fully occur. Some traditional parish churches continue to flourish and evolve with the culture. My guess is that, in the countryside, both traditional expressions and fresh expressions will experience some change and growth and some dying as we learn what sort of church the mission of God requires us to become.

The subheading advertised for my mission seminar is a heart cry for some traditional churches in the countryside where the congregation has dwindled: 'Is new life possible for dying Christian communities?' The answer is not simple. Sometimes God breathes new life into a church. Sometimes God calls its members to let go. In general, there needs to be permission for failure in a climate of learning for old and new together and support for the dying as well as the new born. The Methodist report *Presence* helpfully recognizes the reality of church building closure and offers ways of celebrating the past and moving forward with hope in such circumstances:

> The closure of a traditional building can be the opportunity to develop new patterns of presence. A presence focused on the village hall, school, in homes or in the buildings of other denominations are all possibilities that need to be explored. There may already be an alternative pattern of Christian presence ... Can we offer them the recognition, fellowship, oversight and discipline of the wider church?[5]

Fresh expressions, too, need recognition that things do not always work out as was hoped. When people have invested so much in church planting, it is hard enough for it not to grow without the weight of false guilt.

Alongside the pain we can expect joy. Some models of church will continue to connect as rural culture continues to change and will develop, flourish and bear fruit, just like the seed in the Parable of the Sower (Matthew 13.3-23; Mark 4.2-20; Luke 8.5-15).

Sunday 4.6

Church Army Evangelist Mandy Wright is based at Holsworthy deanery in rural Devon, where the attendance in each parish church averages at just 13. She comments, 'I quickly realized that if the evangelism I was undertaking actually paid off, I would be faced with the difficulty of where to send these people who aren't really looking for traditional church.'[6] Responding to locally felt needs for a chance to 'be ourselves' in worship, Mandy set up 'Sunday 4.6' as an monthly evening service where everybody is encouraged to take an active part. The ethos is that having a go is more important than getting it right. The service would not be considered very 'new' in many areas but here it is a real innovation.

At one meeting each person took a flower from a bunch and put it in a vase whilst saying what they were thankful for. A non-churchgoer who had suffered a stroke and had lost the power of speech got up and very slowly forced the words out: 'Thank you for life.' At another meeting, after Ignatian-style imaginative prayer, a lady who had attended church all her life said that she had met Christ for the very first time during that meditation.

Sunday 4.6 forms an inclusive expression of church which simultaneously builds up people of varied Christian traditions to continue with church involvement elsewhere and allows non-churchgoers to explore faith in a place they can feel they belong.[7]

One feature of many rural fresh expressions of church, such as Sunday 4.6, is the synergy that is created with the parish-based forms. As we move into a truly mixed economy, it can be hoped that one day we will no longer think in terms of two major categories of 'fresh expressions' and 'inherited mode', but that the creative relationships between the two will lead to a whole spectrum of truly inculturated expressions of church in the countryside, sharing the harvest.

Reaping and keeping

A predominent paradigm of conversion and church life offered for much of the twentieth century was one of salvation based on belief (reaping).[8] As consumerism has advanced in the wider culture, this approach has tended to contribute to less emphasis on the importance of ongoing discipleship in community, with churches resorting more to attractional tactics to get uncommitted believers to attend church (keeping). This is a very different situation from that of Jesus' disciples whose faith had led them to leave everything to follow him, long before they were sure of what they believed.

There is a temptation, perhaps particularly in rural areas, to limit mission to pastoral care and seeker-friendly events. Events give the church the warm feeling of being at the heart of the community and often generate funds too. Such events and seeker-type services are a part of evangelistic mission but only a small part – a sort of 'spiritual advertising'[9] – since they do not necessarily give people a real opportunity to explore the questions of faith at a deeper level. They are often very time consuming for clergy so that once the round of such events is completed in all the villages within a multi-parish benefice, there is little energy left to resource moving on in other levels of discipleship. The apostolic church is sent by Christ as he is sent by the Father'[10] and this includes the Great Commission to make disciples (Matthew 28). One of the challenging tasks for all church communities and their leaders is to share in ministry so that discipleship is enabled and encouraged at every level. This is particularly challenging for small churches sharing a minister with others. Unless it is very carefully thought and prayed through, the paid minister is likely to spend a very substantial amount of time performing all of the more visible roles of the traditional country parson multiple times over in each parish, while letting the more hidden responsibilities for the spiritual growth of the flock be marginalized. Whoever practically enables this discipleship, it must be restored at the heart of church life if we wish to be authentically part of Christ's Church. The disciplines of Christian faith are deeply countercultural and require sacrifices but the harvest is reaped and kept in following them.

Learning to do different again

> We need to stop selling worship as a consumer commodity
> and discover discipleship as a countercultural lifestyle.

These words, spoken by a very impassioned Paul Thaxter of the Church Missionary Society, have stayed with me now for over a year. Perhaps it is because, as the incumbent of a rural benefice, I can still expect to gain numbers from special services and there is a temptation to fill the pews a few times a year, whether or not it leads to a deeper discipleship. Perhaps it is because I find it comforting when resources for worship are scarce and I realize that if regarded as a 'consumer commodity' our worship in underheated buildings does not always 'make the grade'. Those who gather week by week come for deeper reasons. Most of all, I think it is because walking the road of discipleship with the people I love in this part of rural England is the hardest and the most joyful thing.

Often, people coming to Christian faith for the first time have no idea of how to pray, read the Bible or the most basic Christian disciplines. I've realized how much I've often taken for granted and have needed to learn again how to start from where people are. I've realized that I can short-change people, if I avoid earthing the challenge to pick up our cross to follow him in this part of rural England. I'm still learning to be a mission-shaped priest. However, I'm not learning alone. Together, we are learning to pattern our lives after the life of Jesus and to experience his power. Together, we are dying to live.

Appendix 1: Recommendations for rural mission-shaped dioceses from the *Mission-shaped Church* report

The recommendations of the *Mission-shaped Church* report – comments and suggestions from one rural practitioner's perspective

This appendix gathers together in one place the recommendations (numbers are given in square brackets) from the *Mission-shaped Church* report that are relevant to diocesan strategy in dioceses with significant rural populations. Under many of the recommendations I offer some suggestions, questions and sources of information about practical implications for the rural context – particularly where I suspect that the recommendation may need to be applied in a significantly different way to help rural multi-parish benefices. There are, of course, many different ways to follow through the recommendations of the *Mission-shaped Church* report and these suggestions are by no means exhaustive – but I hope it will be a useful resource in shaping diocesan mission strategy for rural areas.

Diocesan strategy[1]

Mission-shaped Church should be studied in each diocese and at diocesan synods with a view to helping shape diocesan, deanery and parish mission strategy. [1]

In each diocese, there should be a strategy for the encouragement and resourcing of church-planting and fresh expressions of church, reflecting the network and neighbourhood reality of society and of mission opportunity. [2]

How can a strategy for the encouragement and resourcing of church-planting and fresh expressions reflect the particular mission opportunities offered by the rural context?

(a) within the current bounds of multi-parish benefices

Perhaps, for example, through access to good practical and legal advice for rural congregations which are too small to contain all these skills to enable them to find the best way to put their ideas into practice and to access funds.

Perhaps through help to simplify the structures of a multi-parish benefice in order to make more space for mission. (On the Fresh Expressions' web site, there is a summary of a way by which PCCs in a multi-parish benefice might seek to become united as part of a benefice mission strategy.)

(b) addressing wider network realities in the countryside

For example, through planting of churches at diocesan or regional levels such as a church for the network of the farming community in a region; a regional/deanery rural youth church; or a fresh expression focused on a rural pursuit such as rambling or climbing.

In each diocese an appropriate member of the senior staff should be identified who will be responsible for encouraging, reviewing and supporting existing and developing church plants and fresh expressions of church, and their integration into the ministry of the diocese as a whole. [3]

How will church plants and fresh expressions of church be encouraged, reviewed and supported? Will the senior staff member responsible have time to support a large number of smaller initiatives that may arise in rural areas – or are others sharing the task?

How will church plants and fresh expressions of church gain authorized status and be integrated into the ministry of the diocese as a whole? On the Fresh Expressions' web site there is an article entitled, 'Legal options for the Authorisation of rural Fresh Expressions as Churches' which gives some of the legal options which are available at the time of writing.[2] Other options may be offered by the new 'Diocese, Pastoral and Mission Measure' anticipated to come into force some time in 2006.

The four principles (below) should be adopted (to guide the diocesan response to new mission opportunities):

A   **In any proposed mission where new churches beyond parish boundaries are in view, it is both right and necessary that the**

bishop act as the broker in discussions, with the ability to authorize a new venture or to deny it permission to proceed.

B   Proposed fresh expressions of church need to work in ways that are complementary to inherited ways.

C   Existing ecclesiastical legal boundaries should be seen as permeable.

D   An agreed process is needed to make these values credible. [4]

Deaneries have the potential to bring together a range of human and financial resources, to consider mission across parish boundaries and to share in prayer and encouragement. Each diocese should consider whether its deanery arrangements are best organized and employed to encourage the mission of the Church, particularly among people in cultures and networks not currently connected with church. [5]

Where rural networks overlap such that it is not possible for a deanery's boundaries to be made significantly more meaningful for mission than they are already, how easy is it for neighbouring rural parishes to co-operate across deanery and even diocesan boundaries where this makes the best mission sense?

Breaking New Ground in 1994 contained guidelines for a staged process of transition to maturity and legal recognition for church plants. The latest version of these guidelines and the good practice they reflect should be adopted by each diocese. [6]

The guidelines to which this refers form Appendix I of *Breaking New Ground*, GS 1099, Church House Publishing, 1994. However, they were written with traditional congregation-based church plants in mind and have not yet been thoroughly rewritten to reflect a whole range of fresh expressions in different contexts. They may be found on www.encountersontheedge.org.uk [3] This web site also has an adapted version of those guidelines, made jointly by the original author George Lings and myself with the needs of rural fresh expressions of church in mind.

An appropriate process of record keeping should be established in each diocese, so that church plants and fresh expressions of church can be identified, supported and affirmed and good practice and experience can easily be shared. [7]

Ecumenical collaboration[4]

Local ecumenical co-operation is crucial to the Church's mission. Churches need a light touch process that enables local mission experiments and partnerships between Christians of different denominations. A new category of 'locally negotiated ecumenical partnership' (or equivalent terminology) should be created. [9]

The *Mission-shaped Church* report recommends that dioceses develop their mission strategies with ecumenical collaboration,[5] but it is not intended that this should be a brake on developing strategy. In my own experience, this sort of 'light touch' is already seen in many rural areas, where there is already much informal ecumenical co-operation on the ground and many a PCC relies on members who are actually members of other denominations but choose to support the village church.

How can local churches of different denominations work together most effectively for rural mission?[6]

How can the denominations collaborate more widely for example in training for mission?[7]

Leadership and training[8]

A focus on cross-cultural evangelism, church-planting and fresh expressions of church ... should be a significant feature of Continuing Ministerial Education from ordination through to years 3 and 4. [10]

First curacy posts should be established where church planting skills, gifting and experience can be nurtured, developed and employed. [12]

Incumbency or equivalent posts should be identified where the gifts of church planters can be valued and expressed. [12]

Dioceses should [play their part as part of a national policy to] develop vocational pathways for the identification, deployment, support and training of people with gifting in church planting, evangelism and fresh expressions of church [14] ... A pattern should develop that provides training as part of a process of discernment-for-authorization, rather than training subsequent to discernment, or the removal of existing leaders for training elsewhere.

- A pattern of training, mentoring and apprenticeship should be developed 'on the job', rather than outside or apart from the mission situation where the leader (or potential leader) is exercising their ministry. [15]

- Patterns of authorization for a specific task should be developed (for example, as leader of a church plant) rather than authorization with the assumption of a potentially lifelong ministry. [16]

How will church-planting experience, gifts and training opportunities be sought and identified in rural as well as urban and suburban contexts?

Resources[9]

There is an urgent need to release resources to sustain mission initiatives to the non-churched. The resources of the Church of England are understandably but disproportionately invested in traditional styles of church, which are no longer adequate for mission to the whole nation. Strategies are needed to establish new resources and transfer some existing resources for new initiatives.

In what particular ways are resources 'understandably but disproportionately invested in traditional styles of church, which are no longer adequate for mission' to the rural scene? How will new resources be established and some existing resources transferred for new rural initiatives?

My personal experience would suggest that it is the care of church buildings and the considerable effort and fundraising which is required to maintain them in which we 'disproportionately invest' the resources (financial and practical) of the rural church. If this is the case, key questions for rural areas include:

(a) How can we better use church buildings for rural mission?

(b) Where the PCC's care of the church building or church ruin becomes too much for PCC members and/or actually detrimental to the mission of a church, how can the church building be made redundant?

The Pastoral Measure due to be published in 2006 will allow parts of church buildings to be leased under faculty for wider community use. Where PCCs are too small or infirm to be able to take proper responsibility for their building, a solution where a church is made redundant for community use, and immediately relicensed for worship, may be helpful to allow the building to remain open for worship and creatively used by the wider community. A document on the Fresh Expressions' web site, entitled 'Processes for the creation of a community centre in a church building which is also licensed for worship', may be helpful here.[10]

Appendix 2: Resources

Useful books and reports

Gerald A. Arbuckle, *Earthing the Gospel: An inculturation handbook for pastoral workers*, Geoffrey Chapman, 1990

Archbishops' Commission on Rural Areas, *Faith in the Countryside*, Churchman Publishing, 1990

Churches' Regional Commission for Yorkshire and the Humber, *Sowing the Seed: Church and rural renaissance in Yorkshire and the Humber*, Churches Regional Commission for Yorkshire and the Humber Ltd, October 2003

Church Heritage Forum, *Building Faith in our Future*, Church House Publishing, 2004

Countryside Agency, *The State of the Countryside 2020*, Countryside Agency Publications, 2003

Stephen Croft *et al.*, *Evangelism in a Spiritual Age*, Church House Publishing, 2005

Leslie Francis and Jeremy Martineau, *Rural Visitors: A parish workbook for welcoming visitors in the country church*, ACORA, 2001

Richard Giles, *Re-pitching the Tent: Reordering the church building for worship and mission*, Canterbury Press, 1996

Margaret Hepplethwaite, *Base Communities: An introduction*, Geoffrey Chapman, 1993

Steve Hollinghurst, Yvonne Richmond, Roger Whitehead with Janice Price and Tina Adams, *Equipping your Church in a Spiritual Age: A workbook for local churches*, Group for Evangelisation, 2005

George G. Hunter III, *The Celtic Way of Evangelism: How Christianity can reach the West again*, Abingdon Press, 2000

Bob Jackson, *The Road to Growth: Towards a thriving Church*, Church House Publishing, 2005

Bob Jackson, *Hope for the Church*, Church House Publishing, 2002

J. Martineau, L. J. Francis and P. Francis (eds), *Changing Rural Life: A Christian response to key rural issues*, Canterbury Press, 2004

Methodist Church, *Presence: A workbook to help promote and sustain an effective Christian presence in villages*, The Methodist Church, 2004

Ann Morisey, *Journeying Out: A new approach to Christian mission*, Morehouse, 2004

Stuart Murray, *Church after Christendom*, Paternoster, 2004

Lesslie Newbigin, *The Gospel in a Pluralist Society*, SPCK, 1989

Mike Riddell, *Threshold of the Future: Reforming the Church in the Post-Christian West*, SPCK, 1999

Seeds in Holy Ground: A workbook for rural churches, ACORA, 2005

Ray Simpson, *Church of the Isles: A prophetic strategy for renewal*, Kevin Mayhew, 2003

Tom Sine, *Mustard Seed versus McWorld: Reinventing Christian life and mission for a new millenium*, Monarch, 1999

Lawrence Singlehurst, *Loving the Lost: The principles and practice of cell church*, Kingsway, 2001

Aylward Shorter, *Towards a Theology of Inculturation*, Geoffrey Chapman, 1988

Geoff Treasure, *First the Blade: Growing churches in rural communities*, CPAS, 2002

Short booklets and magazines

Country Way: Life and faith in rural Britain quarterly magazine published by the Arthur Rank Centre

Graham Cray, *Youth Congregations and Emerging Church*, Grove Evangelism series 57, 2002

Steven Croft, *Moving on in a Mission Shaped Church*, Fresh Expressions, 2006

Steven Croft, Claire Dalpra and Geoge Lings, *Starting a Fresh Expression*, Fresh Expressions, 2006

Bob Hopkins (ed.), *Cell Stories as Signs of Mission*, Grove Evangelism series 51, 2000

George Lings, *A Rocha: Christians, conservation and the community*, Encounters on the Edge 26, Sheffield Centre, 2005

George Lings, *Joining the Club or Changing the Rules?*, Encounters on the Edge 5, Sheffield Centre, 2000

George Lings, *Leading Lights: Who can lead new churches?*, Encounters on the Edge 9, Sheffield Centre, 2001

George Lings, *Northumbria Community: Matching monastery and mission*, Encounters on the Edge 29, Sheffield Centre, 2006

George Lings, *Rural Cell Church*, Encounters on the Edge 28, Sheffield Centre, 2005

George Lings *The Village and Fresh Expressions: Is rural different?*, Encounters on the Edge 27, Sheffield Centre, 2005

Stuart Murray and Anne Wilkinson Hayes, *Hope from the Margins: New ways of being church*, Grove Evangelism series 49, 2000

Peter Price, *To Each in their Place*, New Way of Being Church Resource Booklet 3, New Way Publications, 2001

DVDs

Expressions: The DVD 1: Stories of church for a changing culture, Fresh Expressions, 2006

Useful websites

Agriculture and Theology Project – www.agriculture-theology.org.uk
networking for biblically transformed agriculture

Alternative Worship – www.alternativeworship.org
links to worldwide alternative worship sites and access to resources

Anglican Cell Church Network – www.accn.org.uk
a network resource for Anglican churches in the UK that are thinking about
or implementing cell church

Anglican Church Planting Initiatives – www.acpi.org.uk
advice, coaching and consultancy to Anglicans and others on church-planting

A Rocha – www.arocha.org
Christians in Conservation

Arthur Rank Centre – www.arthurrankcentre.org.uk
national centre for rural ministry, serving the rural community and its
churches

Caféplus+ – www.cafeplus.org.uk
the website of a village church's mission initiative

Cell Church UK – www.cellchurch.co.uk
encouraging and promoting relevant cell churches across denominations

Church House Publishing – www.chpublishing.co.uk

Church Missionary Society – www.cms.org.uk
a community of mission service; pioneering mission for over 200 years
encouraging people to live a mission lifestyle, equipping people in mission
service, sharing resources for mission work

Church of England – www.cofe.anglican.org

Community of Saint Aidan and Saint Hilda – www.aidan.org.uk
new monastic community based on roots – rhythms – relationship
resourcing existing churches and looking to plant fresh expressions of church
which model its way of life

Contemplative Fire – www.contemplativefire.org
a fresh expression of church celebrating the sacrament of the present
moment in the beauty of nature, in contemplative liturgy and in teaching of
Jesus and the Christian mystics

Eco-congregations – www.ecocongregation.org
encouraging churches to weave creation care into their life and mission

Encounters on the Edge – www.encountersontheedge.org.uk
site supporting the Encounters on the Edge series of booklets and serving
the Church Army's Sheffield Centre. Additional material to accompany the
Mission-shaped Church report can be found here

Farm Crisis Network – www.farmcrisisnetwork.org.uk
a network based on local groups whose members have a combination of
technical and pastoral understanding to help families in farming and related
activities who are experiencing problems

Fresh Expressions – www.freshexpressions.org
renewing vision, gathering news, supporting growth and developing training
in fresh expressions of church

New Way of Being Church – www.newway.org.uk
encouraging and resourcing church as small communities of people who can
bring transformation to the life of their neighbourhood and workplace

Northumbria Community – www.northumbriacommunity.org
information about this new monastic community, its mission, worship and
resources

Rural Churches Group – www.ruralchurchesgroup.org.uk
a portal to all the rural church networks

Rural Theology Association – www.rural-theology.org.uk
The association aims to: 1. Study the Gospel and develop theology in a rural
setting; 2. Raise awareness of the nature of rural ministry, worship and
mission in the world at large; 3. Discover ways of living in the countryside
which embody a Christian response to the world.

Small Pilgrim Places – www.smallpilgrimplaces.org.uk
bringing new life to small little-used churches, chapels and places of prayer

Glossary of key terms

Church – Within this book 'church' on its own, does not usually refer to an ecclesiastical building. The term 'church building' is used. I have usually used the term 'church' to refer to any Christian ecclesial community that participates in the four marks of church: oneness, holiness, catholicity and apostolicity. It includes both traditional and fresh expressions of church and does not assume a congregational model. I have used the term 'church community' to mean the same thing, where the term 'church' on its own might be misinterpreted to refer to a building or to a particular kind of church. Where 'Church' has been capitalized it refers to the worldwide Church to which these four marks primarily refer in the Creed.

Church planting – the process of starting a new church. The *Mission-shaped Church* report suggests the following definition: 'The process by which a seed of the life and message of Jesus, embodied by a community of Christians is immersed for mission reasons in a particular cultural or geographic context. The intention is that it roots there, coming to life as a new body of Christian disciples well suited to continue in mission.'[11]

Church plant – A church that is the product of a church-planting process

'Dying to live' – poetic shorthand for seeing Jesus' incarnation, death and resurrection as the model for the process of inculturation and church planting

Fresh expression of church – A new or different way of being church in and for our changing culture. This is not a description that fits just any Christian activity or group, but involves a Christian community which is or is on the journey towards becoming a church. A 'fresh expression' may be the result of a church-planting process or it may be the result of a transitional process of inculturation by an existing church that previously took a more traditional form.

Inculturation – the process by which the gospel penetrates to the heart of culture in evangelization, involving a three-way conversation between the existing church (engaging in mission and expressing the gospel in terms of its own culture); the culture outside that church within which the gospel is being shared; and the gospel, bringing challenge and transformation to both conversation partners.

Mixed economy – The principle of denominations valuing and investing both in healthy traditional expressions of church (such as in the Anglican parish or Methodist circuit system) and in fresh expressions of church within their mission strategy.

Network – In the *Mission-shaped Church* report, 'network' refers to a community of people who do not necessarily live in the same geographical location but have a shared culture or social life based on other factors such as work or common interests.

Endpiece

Mission-shaped and Rural is one of a series of books in development to provide resources and support to ministers and churches as they take forward in different ways the ideas contained in *Mission-shaped Church: Church Planting and Fresh Expressions of church in a Changing Context* (Church House Publishing, 2004).

The *Mission-shaped Church* report

Mission-shaped Church was produced by a working party of the Board of Mission and Public Affairs chaired by Graham Cray, Bishop of Maidstone. The report was originally conceived as a follow up to an earlier report on church-planting across the Church of England (*Breaking New Ground*, Church House Publishing, 1994).

To the surprise but delight of the working party which produced it, *Mission-shaped Church* struck a powerful chord across the Church of England, sister churches in the United Kingdom and elsewhere in the world. To date over 20,000 copies have been sold, making it the best selling General Synod report since *Faith in the City* (1984).

Mission-shaped Church was unanimously commended by the Church of England's General Synod in February, 2004. Since then, many of its recommendations have been put into practice and it has been discussed and debated in dioceses, deaneries and parishes.

The *Mission-shaped Church* report coined new language for the range of new developments discovered by the working party: fresh expressions of church. Bishop Graham Cray commented in his presentation of the report to Synod:

The strength of 'fresh expressions' was the direct connection to the Declaration of Assent: the faith 'which the church is called upon to proclaim afresh in each generation'. Our findings show that the challenge to proclaim afresh is no longer primarily a matter of the faithful translation and communication of the gospel but also concerns the very shape of the local church itself.[12]

The arguments and ideas that are summarized in *Mission-shaped Church* have been affirmed and supported by many senior figures in the life of the Church of England, not least the Archbishop of Canterbury. In his presidential address to the Synod in July, 2003, before the report was published, Rowan Williams referred to the strategic moment of opportunity – a *kairos* moment – in the life of the churches:

> . . . we have to ask whether we are capable of moving towards a more 'mixed economy' – recognizing church where it appears and having the willingness and the skill to work with it. Mission, it's been said, is finding out what God is doing and joining in. And at present there is actually an extraordinary amount going on in terms of the creation of new styles of church life. We can call it church planting, 'new ways of being church' or various other things; but the point is that more and more patterns of worship and shared life are appearing on the edge of our mainstream life that cry out for our support, understanding and nurture if they are not to get isolated and unaccountable.[13]

Following the *Mission-shaped Church* report a number of initiatives have been taken at national and diocesan level to resource the Church of England as it moves towards the realities of becoming a mixed economy church: fresh expressions of church alongside parish churches and all of them shaped by mission.

- A new National Officer for Evangelism, Paul Bayes, was appointed with a brief for taking forward the recommendations in *Mission-shaped Church*.

- A new Pastoral Measure is under development which will enable the creation and recognition of non-parochial churches by Bishops' order.

- A new Archbishops' initiative – Fresh Expressions – was launched in September 2004 to resource and encourage fresh expressions of church. Fresh Expressions works across the whole of the Church of England and the Methodist Church.

- The Church Commissioners have identified new and increased funding to enable mission initiatives as a permanent stream of funding to dioceses.

- The Ministry Division has developed guidelines for the recognition, training and deployment of ordained pioneer ministers.

- In dioceses, new posts have been created, mission funds established and policies developed to encourage in different ways a range of fresh expressions of church.

- Many different mission agencies have continued to work in partnership with dioceses and Fresh Expressions to resource this movement.

Local initiatives

However, at the heart of this new movement of mission are, undoubtedly, *local* initiatives. There are already hundreds, if not thousands, of these new projects all across the churches. There is a parallel movement within other denominations. For a flavour of the range, depth and diversity of the movement, explore the on-line directory on the Fresh Expressions website (www.freshexpressions.org.uk). You will see that fresh expressions of church are beginning in every tradition and area and in a whole variety of contexts. There are many stories of courage, imagination and love.

Definition of terms

In any new movement, especially one which is more bottom-up than top-down, language continues to develop and evolve. It is therefore important to be careful about terms.

In this series of books, there is a common approach that the Church of England and the Methodist Church are now committed to developing a mixed economy – fresh expressions of church alongside traditional local churches – and are working together towards this goal.

Traditional local churches are a vital part of our mission. The evidence we have suggests that they are effective in being able to reach out to up to 40 per cent of the population (although this proportion is much lower among the under 40s and in some areas). It is vital that every local church becomes more and more mission shaped. Some of the volumes in the series focus on this aspect of our calling, which remains vital.

Fresh expressions of church are also vital. We need different fresh expressions of church in order to engage effectively with the more than 60 per cent of the population who are beyond the reach of traditional local churches. Establishing fresh expressions of church demands a willingness for the church culture to be shaped to some degree by the culture it is trying to reach. It also demands a willingness to listen to the Spirit in each place to discern the right starting place and way forward: there can be no blueprint.

> **A fresh expression of church is a new and/or different way of being church in and for our changing culture**
>
> Examples include youth congregations; new initiatives in schools; midweek or additional Sunday services; midweek groups for children; network focused congregations, cells; or churches arising from community initiatives – but there are many more.
>
> A fresh expression of church is not normally seen just as an additional activity or simply a stepping-stone for people to Sunday services but as something with the potential to be or become church for those who take part.

It's vital not to set traditional style churches and fresh expressions of church against each other as if they were in competition. The opposite of a fresh expression of church is not a 'stale' expression but a mature Christian community.

Many fresh expressions of church have a journey still ahead of them to maturity. Not all the marks or elements of the church are yet present at this stage of the journey. Many, for example, may take time to develop a sacramental life. Many take time to work through levels of connexion and accountability to the wider church structures.

Many questions

In adopting and commending the report, *Mission-shaped Church*, the Church of England took an important step forward in its understanding of God's mission. That step is itself just part of the long journey in which the whole church has been caught up since the day of Pentecost: the adventure of bearing witness to the risen Christ in the power of the Spirit to the ends of the earth and the end of time. It is the kind of journey, however, which keeps on opening up new questions. This book and others in the series are designed to resource our thinking, reflection and action as the journey continues.

Notes

About the book

1. Rowan Williams, in *Changing Rural Life: A Christian response to key rural issues*, J. Martineau, L. J. Francis and P. Francis (eds), Canterbury Press, 2004, p. 225.

Prologue

1. Archbishop Rowan Williams, Presidential Address to the General Synod, July 2003, www.archbishopofcanterbury.org/sermonsandspeeches/2003. The phrase 'mixed economy' refers to old and new forms of church, alongside each other, within the Church of England.
2. *Mission-shaped Church*, GS 1523, Church House Publishing, 2004, pp. 120ff.

Chapter 1

1. *Mission-shaped Church: Church planting and fresh expressions of church in a changing context* – a report from a working group of the Church of England's Mission and Public Affairs Council, GS 1523, Church House Publishing, 2004.
2. Tim Dearborn, *Beyond Duty: A passion for Christ, a heart for mission*, MARC, 1998, quoted in *Mission-shaped Church*, p. 85.
3. Bob and Mary Hopkins, 'Reaching a lost generation: Lessons from church planting', *Church of England Newspaper*, July 2005; see www.eauk.org/leaders-digest/edition29/hopkins-and-churchplanting.cfm-
4. *Mission-shaped Church*, p. 85. See also *Eucharistic Presidency*, Church House Publishing, 1997, section 2.13, pp. 16–17.
5. For a fuller account see Pete Grieg, *Awakening Cry*, Silver Fish/Novio Publishing, 1998, pp. 43–5.
6. M. Dhavamony, 'The Christian theology of inculturation', *Studia Missionalia* 44, 1995, p. 39.
7. See Lamin Sanneh, *Translating the Message: The missionary impact on culture*, Orbis, 1989.
8. *Mission-shaped Church*, p. 89.
9. John Paul II, Post Synodical Exhortation, 'Ecclesia in Africa', para. 61 (September 1995).
10. *Mission shaped-Church*, p. 90 and *Eucharistic Presidency*, section 2.28.
11. Tom and Christine Sine, *Living on Purpose*, Monarch, London, 2002, p. 58. See also Luke 4.16-21; Isaiah 61.1-2; Luke 7.22; Isaiah 35.1-7; Isaiah 25.6-10.
12. *Mission-shaped Church*, p. 87.
13. As in the *Mission-shaped Church* report, references to an 'incarnational principle' refer to the culturally specific nature of Christ's Incarnation as a pattern for Christian mission, rather than the unique nature of Christ's Incarnation for our

salvation. See *Mission-shaped Church*, Chapter 5 n. 16.

14. Justin Martyr, *Second Apology* 13, trans. Henry Bettenson, *The Early Christian Fathers: A selection from the writings of the Fathers from Clement of Rome to St Athanasius,* 1956, Oxford University Press, 1987, p 64.
15. *Mission-shaped Church*, pp. 86–7.
16. This is relative. Harvest is still the best attended service of the year in some rural parishes.
17. From the Introduction to the service of Holy Baptism, *Common Worship: Initiation Services*, Church House Publishing, 1998, p. 19.
18. *Mission-shaped Church*, p. 89.
19. *Mission-shaped Church*, p. 30.
20. See Martin Down, *Building a New Church Alongside the Old*, Kingsway, 2003.
21. Latin *missio* = 'I send'.
22. *Mission-shaped Church*, p. 85. See also *Eucharistic Presidency*, section 2.13, pp. 16–17.

Chapter 2

1. *The State of the Countryside 2020*, p.18.
2. These organizations are the Countryside Agency, Defra, ODPM – Office of the Deputy Prime Minister, the Office for National Statistics and the Welsh Assembly. More detail on the new definitions can be found in The Countryside Agency, *The State of the Countryside 2004*, Annex 1.
3. Defra, *Agriculture in the UK 2002*, 2003, table 2.4.
4. The Rt Revd Graham James, Bishop of Norwich, *Church of England Newspaper*, 11 June 2005.
5. Countryside Agency, *The State of the Countryside 2020*, 2003, pp. 18–19 quoted in *Presence: A workbook to help promote and sustain an effective Christian presence in villages*, Methodist Church, 2004.
6. Countryside Agency, *Leisure Day Visits*, Report of the 2002–3 Great Britain Day Visits Survey, 2004.
7. David S. Walker, 'Private property and public good', in J. Martineau, L. J. Francis and P. Francis (eds), *Changing Rural Life: A Christian response to key rural issues*, Canterbury Press, 2004, p. 83.
8. *Great Britain Day Visitor Survey 2002*, Countryside Council for Wales, Department for Culture for Media and Sport, Scottish National Heritage, Scottish Tourist Board, Forestry Commission, British Waterways, Environmental Agency, Wales Tourist Board, 2003.
9. John Saxbee, 'A country retreat', in *Changing Rural Life*, p. 9.
10. Michael Langrish, 'Dynamics of community', in *Changing Rural Life*, p. 24. Based on ACRE, *Rural Life: Facts and figures*, Action with Communities in Rural England, 1994.
11. Countryside Agency, *The State of the Countryside 2004*, p. 6.
12. Figures quoted in *The State of the Countryside 2004*, pp. 8–9.

13. Nick Spencer, *Parochial Vision: The future of the English parish*, Paternoster, 2004, p. 89.
14. Countryside Agency, *The State of the Countryside 2020*, 2003.
15. *Faith in the Countryside*, Churchman Publishing, 1990, p. 243.
16. This is how the term is used in *Mission-shaped Church*, GS 1523, Church House Publishing, 2004, pp. 104–5.
17. *Mission-shaped Church*, p. 116.

Chapter 3

1. For a more lengthy treatment of the emergence of the concept of 'inculturation' and different approaches to 'culture', see Sally Gaze, 'Saint Paul and inculturation', unpublished MPhil. thesis, Birmingham University, 1998, pp. 1–14.
2. Although the term 'inculturation' was not used, the theological basis for this approach to mission was explored in *Mission-shaped Church*, GS 1523, Church House Publishing, 2004, Chapter 2, pp. 11–18.
3. These stages represent a synthesis of similar accounts given by specialists in this field. See Aylward Shorter, *Towards a Theology of Inculturation*, London, Geoffrey Chapman, 1988, pp. 56, 63; Onwubiko Enugu, *Theory and Practice of Inculturation, Christian Mission and Culture in Africa*, Snaap Press, 1992, pp. 39–71; A. A. Roest-Crollius, 'What's so new about inculturation?' *Gregorianum* 59,1978, pp. 721–37.
4. 'Mardle' is a Norfolk dialect word meaning 'chat' or 'converse'.
5. Bob Jackson, *Hope for the Church: Contemporary studies for growth*, Church House Publishing, 2002, p. 54.
6. Anthony Russell, *The Country Parson*, SPCK, 1993, p. 161.
7. Anthony Russell, *The Country Parson*, p. 1.
8. Peter Brierley (ed.), *UK Christian Handbook Religious Trends No. 5: The Future of the Church*, Christian Research, 2005.
9. Mission-shaped Church. Presentation for Diocesan Synods, February 2004.
10. Bob Jackson, *Hope for the Church*, p. 132.
11. Terence Mussen, from the remote farming community of Pyworthy in North Devon, quoted in *Church of England Newspaper*, 10 February 2006, p. 2.
12. 1 March 1988.
13. See the description of cell church on pp. 58–60.
14. From the 1988 Lambeth Conference.
15. www.arocha.org An analysis of the question as to whether A Rocha communities can be fresh expressions of church is found in George Lings, *A Rocha: Christians, conservation and the community*, Encounters on the Edge 26, Sheffield Centre, 2005.
16. www.ecocongregation.org
17. www.hidden-britain.co.uk
18. Peter Boyle, in email to me on 4 August 2005.
19. John Saxbee, 'A country retreat', in J. Martineau, L. J. Francis and P. Francis (eds), *Changing Rural Life: A Christian response to key rural issues*, Canterbury Press, 2004, p. 9.

20. Will New, in email to me in February 2006.
21. www.contemplativefire.org
22. The *Mission-shaped Church* report listed twelve kinds of fresh expressions (not an exhaustive list). Alternative worship communities; Base ecclesial communities; Café church; Cell church; Churches arising out of community initiatives; Midweek congregations; Churches connecting with specific networks; School-linked churches; Seeker church; Traditional church plants; Traditional forms of church inspiring new interest (including new monastic communities); Youth congregations.
23. Jim Mynors, 'Rural rivalry and reconciliation', *Rural-Theology* 50, November 1999. See www.rural-theology.org.uk
24. Devon Rural Strategy, Consultation Draft, November 2002.
25. Churches' Regional Commission for Yorkshire and the Humber, *Sowing the Seed: Church and rural renaissance in Yorkshire and the Humber*, Churches' Regional Commission for Yorkshire and the Humber Ltd, October 2003, p. 29.
26. Churches' Regional Commission for Yorkshire and the Humber, *Sowing the Seed*, p. 30.
27. Churches' Regional Commission for Yorkshire and the Humber, *Sowing the Seed*, pp. 60–61; www.hollybushchristianfellowship.co.uk
28. Actual examples of these kind of initiatives are given in boxes under the section on 'Churches arising from community initiatives' in Chapter 4, pp. 60–61.
29. Ann Morisey, *Journeying Out: A new approach to Christian mission*, Morehouse, 2004, p. 41.
30. Ann Morisey calls these kinds of relationship building: 'bonding social capital', 'bridging social capital' and 'brave social capital'. See *Journeying Out*, Chapter 3 'The Big Idea'.
31. Peter Carruthers, 'God@work.rural', a paper presented at the God@work Conference in the Diocese of Monmouth, May 2003. The complete article can be found at www.agriculture-theology.org.uk. Dr Peter Carruthers is Chairman of Farm Crisis Network and Agricultural Christian Fellowship, and a director of the John Ray Initiative (an educational charity which develops and communicates a Christian understanding of the environment). He works for the Commission for Rural Communities.
32. The *Mission-shaped Church* report is sometimes falsely portrayed as hostile to 'place'. In fact, p. 5 of the report is explicit about not replacing neighbourhood, while showing how the nature of neighbourhood is changing.
33. The Rt Revd Graham James, 'Mission and the parochial shaped Church', paper for the DDOs conference, Swanwick, 8 February 2005.
34. This controversial principle states: 'People like to become Christians without crossing racial/linguistic/class/cultural barriers.' Donald McGravan, *Bridges of God*, Friendship, 1955, quoted in *Mission-shaped Church*, p. 108.
35. 'Rural communities have always provided an important model of how the gospel works: the focus is upon the identity and connections made around a sense of parish and place.' The Rt Revd Alistair L. J. Redfern, 'Listening to the Anglican tradition', in *Changing Rural Life*, p. 249.

36. Walter Brueggemann, *The Land: Place as gift, promise and challenge in biblical faith*, SPCK, 1977, p. 10.
37. Rowan Williams, 'Theological reflections', in *Changing Rural Life*, p. 255.

Chapter 4

1. 'Traditional forms of church inspiring new interest' was presented alongside the other fresh expressions of church in the original *Mission-shaped Church* report. I have wished to spend longer reflecting on this phenomenon in the rural setting and have therefore made it a separate section within the chapter.
2. *Mission-shaped Church*, GS 1523, Church House Publishing, 2004, p. 45.
3. 'The Gathering' is the title of the worship of 'Contemplative Fire', a fresh expression of church in Oxford diocese. For further information, see www.contemplativefire.org
4. The leaders of 'The Gathering' would not use the term 'alt. worship' because of some of the marked differences described above compared to urban forms.
5. John Summers, *A Fresh Start: The story of New Way in an Anglican parish*, New Way of Being Church Resource Booklet 14, New Way Publications, 2003.
6. Peter Price, *To Each in Their Place*, New Way of Being Church Resource Booklet 3, New Way Publications, 2001, contains a 5-step process on pp. 25ff.
7. John Summers, *A Fresh Start: The story of New Way in an Anglican parish.*
8. Revd David Clayden writing in *Country Way: Life and faith in rural Britain* 39, Summer 2005, p. 21.
9. On these cell values see Lawrence Singlehurst, *Loving the Lost: The principles and practice of cell church*, Kingsway 2001.
10. As in the Case of the Tas Valley Cell Church, see Prologue.
11. See pp. xiii–xviii.
12. Another example, which could have been placed in this section, is that of the Discover Dentdale visitors centre at St Andrew's, Dent in Chapter 3, p. 39.
13. A more detailed account may be found in Annette Reed, 'Satellite Post Office and new meeting facilities in Sheepy Magna Church', *Country Way: Life and Faith in Rural Britain* issue 37, Autumn 2004, p. 5.
14. With thanks to Monica Long. A more detailed account may be found in her article 'On the Agenda', *Country Way: Life and faith in rural Britain* issue 37, Autumn 2004, p. 7.
15. More about these parishes can be found at www.beneficeorwell.co.uk
16. www.cherwellvalley.org
17. *Mission-shaped Church*, p. 63.
19. See pp. 40–41.
19. See pp. 42.
20. See pp. xiii–xviii.
21. *Mission-shaped Church*, p. 64.
22. With thanks to the Revd Ian Bentley, rector of the united benefice of Ditchingham, Hedenham, Broome, Earsham, Alburgh and Denton, Diocese of Norwich.

23. As one official from a rural diocese responded to the questionnaire, circulated by the working party of *Mission-shaped Church*, 'With 648 churches in this diocese, there is little incentive to plant more.'

24. The story of the first eight years of 'Stepping Stones' is told in George Lings, *Stepping Stones*, Encounters on the Edge 18, Sheffield Centre, 2003. See also www.anstonstjames.org

25. www.edenzone.com

26. See Stuart Murray, *Church after Christendom*, Paternoster, 2004, Chapter 7.

27. *Faith in the Countryside*, Churchman Publishing, 1990, p. 181 reflecting on the Rural Theology Association's Publication, *The Rural Church Towards 2000*.

28. *Seeds in Holy Ground: a workbook for rural churches*, ACORA publishing, 2005, p. 9.

29. The Right Revd Alistair L. J. Redfern, 'Listening to the Anglican tradition', in J. Martineau, L. J. Francis and P. Francis (eds), *Changing Rural Life: A Christian response to key rural issues*, Canterbury Press, 2004, p. 239.

30. www.worthabbey.net/bbc

31. Ian Corsie, in an email to me in February 2006. More details of the Northumbria community can be found at www.northumbriacommunity.org

Chapter 5

1. *Eucharistic Presidency*, Church House Publishing, 1997, Chapter 2 'The Church in the purposes of the Triune God', p. 20.

2. Paul Avis, *The Anglican Understanding of the Church*, SPCK, 2000, p. 65, quoted in *Mission-shaped Church*, GS 1523, Church House Publishing, 2004, p. 97.

3. *Mission-shaped Church*, Chapter 5, pp. 96–9. I am also indebted to George Lings' on-line commentary on this chapter at www.encountersontheedge.org.uk

4. Five Marks of Mission from the 1988 Lambeth Conference: To proclaim the Good News of the kingdom; To teach, baptise and nurture new believers; To respond to human need by loving service; To seek to transform unjust structures of society; To strive to safeguard the integrity of creation and sustain and renew the earth.

5. See pp 59–60.

6. Threshold: 'The shape we are in 10 years on'. www.thresholdchurch.co.uk September 2005.

7. Threshold: 'The shape we are in 10 years on'. www.thresholdchurch.co.uk September 2005.

8. George Lings, Commentary on Chapter 5 of the *Mission-shaped Church* report.

9. See pp. 69–70.

10. Café*plus*+ brochure available from www.cafeplus.org.uk

11. More on the Cafe*plus*+ story can be found on pp. 87–8.

12. *Mission-shaped Church*, p. 98.

13. See *Mission-shaped Church*, pp. 120–24.

14. The Rt Revd Graham James, 'Mission and the parochial shaped Church', paper for the DDOs conference, Swanwick, 8 February 2005.

Chapter 6

1. Romans 11.17-24. Paul compares God's people to an olive tree rather than a vine in this letter but the significance is the same as the vine analogy.
2. See pp. 10–14 to see the significance of 'dying to live' in a mission-shaped church.
3. N. T. Wright, *John for Everyone Part 2*, SPCK, 2002, p. 67.
4. Nick Spencer, *Parochial Vision: The future of the English parish*, Paternoster, 2004, p. xii.
5. John Saxbee, 'A country retreat', in *Changing Rural Life: A Christian response to key rural issues*, J. Martineau, L. J. Francis and P. Francis (eds), Canterbury Press, 2004, p. 18.
6. Church Heritage Forum, *Building Faith in our Future*, Church House Publishing, 2004, p. 28.
7. Diocese of Norwich, *Church Buildings: A cause of delight and a source of anxiety*, Report of a Working Group of the Diocese of Norwich, November 2003.
8. John Inge, *A Christian Theology of Place*, Ashgate, 2003, p. 91.
9. John Inge, *A Christian Theology of Place*, p. 103.
10. John Inge, *A Christian Theology of Place*, pp. 113–14.
11. By 'churches' John Inge means church buildings.
12. John Inge, *A Christian Theology of Place*, p. 115.
13. Yvonne Richmond, 'A spiritual snapshot', in Stephen Croft *et al.*, *Evangelism in a Spiritual Age*, Church House Publishing, 2005. Some 78 per cent of the adult UK population visit churches each year as tourists.
14. www.smallpilgrimplaces.org.uk
15. John V. Taylor, *Christians and the Holy Places: The myth of Jewish-Christian origins*, Clarendon Press, 1993, p. 2 lists four main categories of religious building – the wayside shrine, the school of religion, the local congregation-church and the major temple-shrine.
16. John Saxbee, 'A country retreat', p. 18.
17. Rural churches need £10,000 average in repair costs each three years, once they have been brought up to a good standard of repair. The average costs of providing disabled access is £49,000 per church. Background Note by Roy Thompson to General Synod Motion 1610A 'The Church's Built Heritage', February 2006.
18. *Country Way* issue 37, 2004, p. 18, citing part of *Faith in the Countryside*, Churchman Publishing, 1990.
19. For many of these observations, I am indebted to George Lings, *Rural Cell Church*, Encounters on the Edge 28, Sheffield Centre, 2005, p. 25.
20. Church Heritage Forum, *Building Faith in our Future*, p. 29.
21. Richard Giles, *Re-pitching the Tent: Reordering the church building for worship and mission*, Canterbury Press, revised edn 1999, p. 59.
22. The energy spent on church buildings is shown by the following statistic from the Background Note prepared by the Cathedral and Church Buildings Division to the General Synod Motion 1610, 'The Church's Built Heritage'. Looking after a Grade 1 listed rural church in Yorkshire with 110 on the electoral roll is estimated to take 9 hours per week for each church warden.
23. Bob Jackson, *Hope for the Church: Contemporary strategies for growth*, Church House Publishing, 2002, p. 4.

24. See D. W. Winnicott, 'Transitional objects and transitional phenomena', in *Collected Papers*, Tavistock, 1958.
25. Gareth Morgan, *Images of Organization*, Sage, 1989, p. 222.
26. *Mission-shaped Church*, GS 1523, Church House Publishing, 2004, p. 120.
27. See Walter Brueggemann, 'Rethinking Church models through Scripture', *Theology Today* 48.2, July 1991.
28. A more detailed account can be found in *Faith in the Countryside*, pp. 138–9, 165–9.
29. *Mission-shaped Church*, p. 120.
30. The formation of a Joint PCC under a pastoral scheme does not mean that separate PCCs are no longer necessary for each parish. Rather, this is an additional structure to which the PCCs may delegate such of their functions as they see fit. For example, it is often useful for a benefice to have some joint funds for mission initiatives and the payment of clergy expenses. See *Church Representation Rules* part II no. 19.
31. District Church Councils.
32. Nick Spencer, *Parochial Vision: The future of the English parish*.
33. John Finney, *Rediscovering the Past: Celtic and Roman mission*, Darton, Longman & Todd, 1996.

Chapter 7

1. Mission 21, Sheffield, March 2006.
2. Ann Morisey, *Journeying Out: A new approach to Christian mission*, Morehouse, 2004, pp. 62–3.
3. Archbishop Rowan Williams at the Mission-shaped Church conference, St Barnabas, Kensington, 23 June 2004.
4. Revd Dr Malcolm Brown, 'Whose Church? Which culture? Discerning the missionary structures for tomorrow', in *A Measure for Measures in Mission and Ministry: Report of the Review of the Dioceses Pastoral and Related Measures*, Church House Publishing, 2004, Appendix 1, p. 122.
5. Methodist Church, *Presence: A workbook to help to promote and sustain Christian presence in villages*, Methodist Church, 2004, p. 41.
6. 'Tomorrow's evangelism today', Part 1, David Coleman, *Church of England Newspaper*, 10 February 2006, p. 10.
7. A fuller account of Sunday 4.6 can be found in George Lings, *The Village and Fresh Expressions: Is rural different?* Encounters on the Edge 27, Sheffield Centre, 2005, pp. 18–28.
8. See Mike Riddell, *Threshold of the Future: Reforming the Church in the Post-Christian west*, SPCK, 1999, Chapter 10 'Finding faith'.
9. George Lings, *The Village and Fresh Expressions: Is rural different?*, p. 25.
10. *Eucharistic Presidency*, Church House Publishing, 1997, Chapter 2 'The Church in the purposes of the Triune God', p. 21.

Appendix 1

1. *Mission-shaped Church*, GS 1523, Church House Publishing, 2004, pp. 145–6.
2. www.freshexpressions.org.uk
3. Guidelines for Dioceses to aid a staged process of transition to maturity and legal recognition for rural church plants.
4. *Mission-shaped Church*, p. 146.
5. *Mission-shaped Church*, p. 145 recommendation no. 2.
6. *Mission-shaped Church*, p. 27.
7. *Mission-shaped Church*, p. 147 no. 13.
8. *Mission-shaped Church*, pp. 147–8.
9. *Mission-shaped Church*, p. 149.
10. www.freshexpressions.org.uk
11. *Mission-shaped Church*, p. 32.
12. Bishop Graham Cray, *Report of Proceedings of the General Synod*, February, 2004, Church House Publishing, 2004, p. 130.
13. Archbishop Rowan Williams, Presidential Address to the General Synod, July, 2003, www.archbishopofcanterbury.org/sermonsandspeeches/2003

Index

Note: An asterisk * following a page number indicates an entry in the Glossary; an 'n' indicates an end note.